WHEN THE DEAD COME CALLING

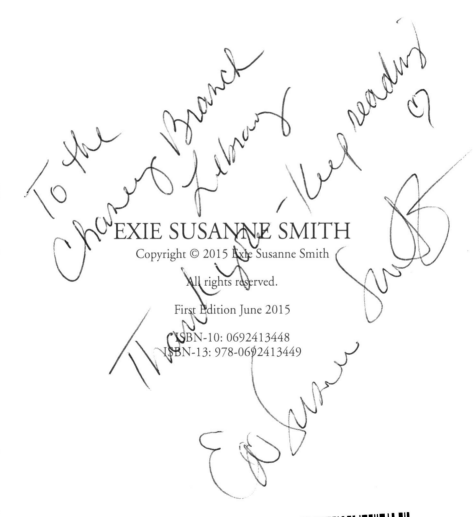

EXIE SUSANNE SMITH

First Edition June 2015

ISBN-10: 0692413448
ISBN-13: 978-0692413449

D1245877

DEDICATION

To my husband and son, thank you for allowing me to follow
my passion.
You have given me an amazing gift.
You mean the world to me.

To my Parents, Mom on Earth and Dad now in Heaven, I
love you.

Louise always my savior, I thank you.

Thank you to everyone who purchased
my first book.
I am humbled and grateful.
You have given me the opportunity to pursue my passion.

ACKNOWLEDGMENT

Cover Art
Kate Cowan of KC Designs

FORWARD

In my first book, Welcome To My Para"Normal" Life, I grouped like similar paranormal events into chapters. This book is presented in the same manner so the events are not necessarily in chronological order. For clarity, I have placed the symbol "###" as a divider between each individual event.

The goal of this book is to help you gain a better understanding of the paranormal. I hope to answer some of your questions and help you realize that you are not alone if you are seeing, hearing and feeling unexplainable phenomena.

I am still discovering new aspects of who I am and how I fit into this paranormal world. I am thankful for my continued growth and experiences. Each event is a learning opportunity. I hope this book helps you understand your experiences and, in turn, eases your travels along life's path.

Thank you for purchasing my book.

CONTENTS

CHAPTER 1

SPIRIT ATTACHMENT

A spirit can attach itself to something or someone. The events in this chapter involve attachments only to objects, not to people. It should be noted that an object does not change in appearance when a spirit is attached to it.

###

This experience was a first for me. Quite honestly, it scared me

My mom and I were attending an artisan jewelry show. There were many beautiful items made of all types of wood, metals and crystals. I was captivated by the talent in the room that could create on this level. We talked with each artist as we walked from table to table. I wanted to under-stand their thought processes, how they decided upon the particular materials they used. I was also curious as to how they knew when a piece of jewelry, or other craft, was finished and complete.

I came upon an interesting table along the wall. It dis-played a collection of what the artist called "Prayer Dolls." With those were her unique wooden boxes with tiny crosses on top. The artist said, "You could put secrets in them."

The boxes interested me, so I reached for one that caught my eye. I tried to pick it up, but my hand was physically stopped just above the box. I looked from my still hovering hand up into the face of the artist. She was staring directly at me with shiny, solid black eyes. The smile on her face had my blood running cold. I felt eerily aware of my situation. My hand snapped away from the table, and my body physically took a step back out into the isle. What I saw in her eyes was shinny solid black.

The woman was amused by my reaction to the box. She looked me up and down, an assessment of sorts. An overwhelming feeling hit me and I almost wretched. I honestly felt as if was going to vomit! She tried to hand me the wooden box. I simply backed away and went to locate my mom.

When I found Mom I said, "Skip the next table with the wood boxes! Do not touch anything made by that artist. I will explain later." When we arrived at the next table, I realized my arm was tingling as if it had been asleep. It was the same arm I used to reach for the wooden box. I was shaken up.

Without any further discussion, we continued our shopping, made our purchases and left the building. We walked down the quaint street for dinner. After I chugged a glass of wine I said to mom, "The table with the boxes and dolls was bad. The boxes felt alive."

"What do you mean by bad and how can they be alive?"

"Mom they were bad, possibly evil, I am not sure. They felt as if someone was living inside them."

"You never use evil as an explanation, I am glad I didn't touch one. How does that happen?

I was not certain I had an answer for her but I tried. "I'm not sure. I think it was intentional though. She is not a good person. I think she put a spell or charm on them. Maybe it was the wood she used to construct the boxes, no telling where it came from."

"What do you mean by that?"

"It could have been made from an old coffin or a piece of furniture, or a picture frame that had a spirit attachment already. She could have called spirits to the objects. Who knows?"

My mom was visibly upset and asked, "To what purpose would she put a spell on them?"

Not being very familiar with the subject, I offered what I thought might be examples of reason to put a spell on an object. I said, "It could be for control reasons, sales, friendship, love, deception or a combination of things. I think she tried to cast a spell on me to get me to hold one of the boxes. She looked at me oddly, from head to toe, and then I felt ill. She tried to hand me a box. I think most people would have unknowingly taken the box from her." My mom was shocked that any and all of this even exists.

I thought about this event for several days. It bothered and intrigued me. Was it possible that the artist was also a victim of the items she was selling? I may never know but I am glad none of her items ended up in my home!

###

A new spirit showed up in the house recently. It was hard to miss; it had an "odd in your face" feel. My impression is that this spirit knows about my gift and is thumbing its nose at me. Who was this? Where did it come from? Why is it here? I needed answers.

I retrace my steps over the last week. What had I done to attract this entity? Where had I been that something might have followed me home or attached to me? Had I brought anything new into my home? Anything old?

The last question got my attention. I went down the hall to look at an old family photo I had brought home from my parents condominium basement. I was helping them move some things around when I saw this photo. I asked my dad if I could have it. He said, "Sure, it just sits here in the basement, we never display it."

In my first book, "Welcome To My Para"Normal Life," I described an experience I had in the basement of my parent's condo. They were preparing for a garage sale and asked for my help. I was carrying things up from the basement when my flip flop was held down to the floor. I could not lift it up to the bottom step. I looked to see if someone was behind me, no one. I recognized there was a spirit present but I did not know who it was. I have to admit I always felt watched in their basement.

In the hallway looking at the old picture and thinking, when this photograph was taken just after turn of the last century, people posed with stoic expressions. My grandmother's image looked as it should be in a photo, lifeless and flat. However the image of my great-uncle, appeared brighter and seemed to have depth. I looked even closer at the photo and asked him, "Did you come attached to the photo?" Not getting or expecting an answer, I want on with my day.

So many strange things have happened in this house. I am accustom to paranormal experiences and generally accept them without explanation. In this case, however, I was convinced that what I was seeing, hearing and feeling was all tied to that old family portrait. A few nights after my conversation with my great uncles image, I received confirmation that his spirit was indeed in our home!

We had just gotten into bed, our dog Lola had stayed in the living room. Reaching for the television remote on the nightstand to shut the TV off, I felt the covers being yanked, twice from below the edge of the bed. I quickly got up to see what this could have possibly been. Funny that I was actually surprised when there was nothing there. Back in bed, it happened again, yank, yank on the covers. Jumping out of bed again, trying to catch the spirit who was doing this, nothing. Thank the Lord my husband slept on, I do not like spirits to bother him.

I needed separation from this so I left the room, I thought I would check on our Lola to make sure she was all right and get a drink of water. I also took a moment to have a conversation aloud to who ever thought this was cute. I wanted them to know, it was not.

Seeing Lola was fine, I sat on the couch with my water and said, "This is our home, you are bothering us. The room you were in is a sanctuary, no bothersome spirits or ghosts are allowed."

Next, I spoke directly to my Spirit Guide, "Please assist me in making sure our home is safe from bothersome spirits and to figure out who this is. I don't like the feeling I get from this spirit, it feels unbalanced, possibly mentally insane."

When I am around someone with a mental illness, it feels and sounds like static, the kind when a television station goes off the air, noise and all.

The message I got my spirit guide was expected. She said, "Yes it is your Great Uncle and he did come attached to the portrait."

Spirit attachment is new to me; I am honestly not sure what to do about him and the portrait, the object of his attachment.

The weird thing is I only brought the portrait home because it has my grandmother in it. Although he is a relative, I never met him. My father did tell me wonderful stories of him, he sounded like a great guy and possibly a prankster, lovely! My dad also touched on the subject of his sad painful death. The last time my dad saw him, he said his Uncle had half his face covered with a cloth. He didn't want him to see the ravages of his sinus cancer. My dad said even with the cloth covering, it was bad, something he could not forget. Consequently, it is a story that will stick with me as well.

Great Uncle Bub, as my dad called him, had been one of the Rough Riders who chased after Poncho Via. Once Via was capture, they shipped his division off to fight in Europe, WWI. He was one of many who were unfortunate enough to have been in the trenches when mustard gas canisters were dropped in. Years after the war, came the diagnosed of sinus cancer, stemming from the exposure to the mustard gas. His particular faith does not prescribe to the care of doctors, he kept to his faith.

After hearing details of his death, the possibility of insanity made sense. With the belief that what you are in life, you are in death, I assumed he had become insane before dying. I do not know this as fact but believed it to be true at the time of the journal entry.

At this juncture, I was heavily considering taking the portrait back to my parent's basement. Then I would be done with it. He was draining my energy and my patience. Plus, my son disliked the portrait from the minute I brought it into the house. Besides his spirit seemed to be fine all those years hanging out in the basement.

Instead, I decided to have a "Come to Jesus" conversation with him and see what happened.

"Hello. I know you hear me and understand I am talking to you and I know I have your attention. I am tired of being toyed with. Do you understand who I am to you, family relations wise? I am not simply someone who ended up with your photograph, a stranger. I am your great niece. I am your much loved sister's granddaughter."

I could feel his surprise and was on a roll so I kept going. "We, you and I, are family. Stop being such an immature jerk of a spirit, grow up!" I smiled and could tell he had not. "I know how much you loved my dad, your nephew, and he you. I know too that you were in the basement all those years, left to yourself. However you are now in my home, so follow the rules or get out. It is up to you, at this point, I do not care either way."

I meant that and felt he knew I did as well. "I have that photo with you in it to honor and remember my grandmother, you are inconsequential." I felt a bit of guilt for being that brutally honest but he had pushed me to my limit.

Right after I stopped talking I heard a strange vocal sound, coming from in the house, but could not make out what was said. Was it acceptance or screw you?

In the days that followed this semi one sided conversation the house was calm feeling. This pleased me; maybe he got the message about being family being kind and good to one another.

In the early morning of the third day, after the conversation, I was awakened by the sound of a crying child, yelling for help. Coming out of a deep sleep, I knew what I was hearing was real. Rushing out of bed, I checked in the house and out, no one was around. In my gut I knew I was not going to find anyone.

Standing silently in the middle of my house I concentrated on the voice, the tone and lilt. That was not a voice from this era or plane. Having watched many old movies this voice sounded to be out of the 1920s or 1930s.

I do get spirits in my life that drop in at will, so not sure I can actually credit my great uncle with this. I asked my spirit guide and she said, "It was your great uncle, he is unhappy with you and how you talked to him. His punishment was to get you up early."

Thanking my spirit guide, I got coffee and sat with my lap-top to research this man on the internet. I think I should have done this sooner.

I knew he had lived in California and had adopted a male child but that was it. I thought I should start with social networking and his last name. I found someone on there, in California and about the age I thought the person should be. Plus his first name was my dad's middle name. I sent him a message. Bull's-eye, this person was his grandson, I had found my second cousin.

In my message to this man, my relative, I dropped some hints in the direction of spirits and hauntings. I wanted to test the water, so to speak, before I dropped the information that his grandfather's spirit was not only in my house but camped out in my attic.

Putting this out in a note my stomach churned but was unfounded. His note in return was one of acceptance, I was impressed and relieve.

In the next message he brought up a scrap book that his grandfather had put together. He wanted me to have it. Since he was adopted, he thought it should be with someone in the natural line.

I replied, "You are a family member as much as I am, this is silly."

He said, "I have never felt that way and would like you to have it, please."

With that reply I felt as if I could not say no and typed in my address.

Days later a well aged black leather scrap book was delivered to my home. Inside were pictures of my great uncle and his fellow Rough Riders on the boarder chasing after Poncho

Villa. Next came photos of him in a boot camp in Michigan getting ready to ship out, bound for France and the trenches of WWI. In the back ground of his pictures in boot camp, he wrote about the new machine called an "Aeroplane."

After going through all the post cards, pictures and news clippings I sat to digest this amazing history lesson.

I sent a note of thanks to my new cousin in California and included a copy of my first book. A gift for a gift, if you will. Weeks later my cousin called me my on the phone. I tried one more time to get him to take the scrap book back, he would not have it. I thanked him and told him that everyone that we showed was blown away. He talked about his grandfather, "He was an honorable and courageous man."

Then he brought up my book, "I am impressed by your book and amazed by your gift. In the book the part where you had the spirit alarm clock wake you up. That made me think of something my grandfather use to do to wake me up in the morning. He would come in my room and tug on my covers just below the top of the mattress." With a chuckle he said, "If this happens to you, let me know!"

I said, "Thanks for the warning but it's too late, it already has." We both laughed.

Disconnecting with him, my son who had been near said,

"You don't remember?"

"Remember what?"

"Mom, I told you weeks ago that something or someone had tugged on the covers at the foot of my bed!" He was right, I had totally forgotten.

After I spoke with my cousin that day, the energy in the house was peaceful, void of static. We are all connected and things had fallen into place. A spirit that had been happily dormant for years awoke. It all came down to a moment in time, no, the moment in time. The moment it was all supposed to happen in.

When I first received this scrap book, I showed it to my dad. He said, "It is as it should be daughter. After all you are the keeper of the family history!

During these events, I learned an extraordinary amount of information. This was more than a family history lesson, it was a lesson about family ties that bind, about love and bravery even unto death. About not jumping to conclusions and about pain, physical and mental.

I have been gifted with a beautiful family and a mystifying life. Thank you, thank you, thank you.

###

CHAPTER 2

GHOSTS AND SPIRITS AT HOME

Love the gift of "girlfriend time" with my dear friend. She is a medium along with other God given gifts. We relax, drink wine, share good conversation and occasionally cook dinner together. We have not been able to coordinate our schedules and had a lot to catch up on.

She arrived at my house and we began preparing food for dinner. I was on one side of the island making a salad, she on the other side. Wine poured, we clinked our glasses and were about to take a sip, when something to my left moved. It was a shadow. "Odd," was all I could verbalize. The shadow moved again, in the kitchen sink, of all places. My friend and I were now staring at the sink. The shadow then jumped up out of the sink onto the counter, and then off onto the floor. I whipped around and asked, "Did you see that? Was it simply a hunk of lettuce falling?"

She said, "What lettuce? That was a dark shadow that came up behind you and jumped into the sink."

All I could do was stare at her. She had been watching a shadow behind me, just before I saw it.

She said, "You caught sight of it as it went into the sink and then jumped out. Where did it go after that?" I replied, "It jumped onto the counter then off toward the floor.

As it fell it faded away and disappearing before it hit the floor."

Neither of us had any idea what it was. During dinner we concluded, that when we are together, we stir up a lot of spiritual energy! It was not the first, nor will it be the last, paranormal event we share.

My husband got up for work at about 5:20 a.m. and as usual, I rolled to my side to snuggle with our Schnauzer, Lola. Just as both of us settled, I felt something walking above my head on the pillow. I felt four light and careful steps being taken. There was an indiscernible noise simultaneously with the last step, and then the feeling of a small head tucking into my neck area, between my ear and shoulder. Then I heard a sniffing inhale, and then an exhale of contentment.

I knew it was our past doggy daughter Bailey. She is buried outside our bedroom window in the flower garden. It was so sweet that she wanting to curl up and sleep with me. I did not know this could happen. As I cherished this moment, I relaxed and fell soundly back to sleep.

Later that day when I talked to my husband on the phone, he said, "You were so sound asleep when I kissed you goodbye. The look on your face was so sweet. I didn't have the heart to wake you. Were you dreaming?"

All I could say was no. What could I say, when it was my own special experience? Thank you for the gift Bailey.

###

Little spiritual events have been happening to me at home on such a constant basis that it has become annoying.

My husband and I sat snuggled under a blanket watching television in the living room one night. I turned and reached for my water glass. As I did so I noticed a shadow person on the other side of the small end table. It was not a full shadow person, just the head and shoulders, about 3 feet off the ground. It startled me and I recoiled a bit into my husband's side. We had been holding hands but I let go when I felt the buzz of electricity going through the hand that reached for the glass. I did not want my husband to get shocked or have any ill effects.

Knowing I do not normally react like that, he said, "What the hell did you just see?"

I said, "Shit! There was a partial black shadow, only its head and shoulders, right next to the table! That was unexpected."

The spirit appeared to me in shadow form, another person might see exactly what the spirit looked like. I wonder if spirit chooses the form it wants to be seen in.

This shadow was a lighter shade of black, almost brown, not the same shade as the others I have seen.

Thirty minutes later, my hand was still tingling.

Evening had finally fallen after this particularly marvelous day. I had just finishing eating a wonderful late dinner, and my stomach was full. Feeling content, I decided to sit and read for a while . Unfortunately, I woke up only a few minutes later with the book on my chest. It was time for me to head to bed.

As soon as I crossed the threshold into my bedroom, my senses went on high alert, I was not alone. A spirit popped up in front of me and was very close to my face. It felt as if it was pushing me, trying to pick a fight. My eyes were adjusting to the darkness, but I could see this spirit was male. He had a full face and was partially bald. I ignored him, like I would any bully; I felt he was toying with me. Clothes changed, I went to make sure the back door was lock. I turned around and there he was in my face again! He disappeared quickly. I walked back into the bedroom, BAM! He was in my face, AGAIN!

This was not a particularly scary event to me. I think the spirit meant it to be and that is why he kept trying. The spirit wanted my attention and had it. I was nervous about this event because, in the past, visits of this sort have preceded the arrival of bad news. I was no longer sleepy, so I sat on the edge of the bed and told my husband, "We might be receiving some news tonight or tomorrow and I am thinking not good news. Time will tell."

He said, "Try and get some sleep Honey. Right at this moment there is nothing you can do."

I slept but not deeply.

Baby sitting my phone all morning. It finally rang around noon. I dreaded answering, but did tentatively, "Hello." There was a solemn reply, "Hello." It was my lifelong girlfriend, we had befriended each other in the 4th grade. She had unfortunately learned several months earlier, that she had lung cancer. She had struggled through both chemotherapy and radiation. She had hoped to kick this cancer's ass! As always, I prayed for the best news. That news being her tumors were shrinking. I stayed positive; my heart was racing as I waited for some good news. Had my prayers been answered?

She said, "Hey woman, I wanted to tell you personally what is going on."

"Cool, what is happening?"

She continued, "I was told yesterday that my treatments are no longer working, and this morning I contacted Hospice."

My brains could not comprehend this information. I talked with her for a while, but I do not remember what we talked about. What I do remember is that she had to hang up; Hospice had arrived for their face-to-face meeting. She called back later that day but, again, I do not remember what we talked about.

Between my two conversations with her, I called my husband at work to deliver the awful news. I am a lucky woman to be married to this man. He said, "Well that explains the spirit visit last night. This is sad news. Do you want me to come home now?"

I had totally forgotten about that spirit visit the night before. I said, "No, I will be fine. You are right, though, because I think that was her dad." I love it when things pop out of my mouth before they have cognitively register with my brain. Wait, it was her dad without his hat on. That is why I did not immediately recognize him. My memory always has him in a hat.

Her dad's spirit had come to visit it me years earlier, immediately after he had passed away. During that visit I promised him that I would look out for his daughter for the rest of my life. He came back to remind me of that promise. It was my honor to be her friend.

When my girlfriend called back we made plans for me to visit her often. Unfortunately, that never happened because she had so many family members trying to spend time with her in the days she had left. The day I decided I would just go and try to see her anyway, she passed away. I had a feeling this was going to be the way.

There is a dedication to her in my first book, and I included several paranormal events she shared with me.

I have written before about forbidding spirit in my bedroom. There is an annoying spirit who was coming in our bedroom, all hours of the day and night. It was bothering me, my husband, and our dog. I laid down the law, put a white light of protection around the room, and said, "No spirits… family, friend or otherwise… are allowed in here!" The spirit obeyed and we were able to sleep undisturbed for months. The spirit did come back into my bedroom once and my great uncle popped in for a second too. I yelled, they left.

At times it is easier to ignore my instincts rather than analyze and deal with the paranormal activity in my life. Because of this, I had allowed a new spirit into my bedroom.

He has been standing just to the left of the foot of our bed, in the darkest corner of the room. I know he is there, I feel him. He and I stare across the room at each other in the dark.

Whoever this spirit is, he stays hidden in the corner. I cannot discern shape or color of his shadow. He was not bothering us but is unusually creepy.

He needs to go. I believe this spirit was attached to an object I brought home. He continued to lurk in our bedroom for weeks to come.

The Common feeling in the house now is that there is yet another new spirit here. This one is intentionally staying just out of sight. It arrived several months after the lurking spirit in the bedroom departed.

This time instead of ignoring the spirit, my instinct led me to welcome it and find out who it was. Setting my mind and paranormal gifts on the task, an outline showed up. After a few moments, there was more definition. It was a man in a suit. He would appear for a moment and then fade away. He gave the impression he was having a hard time. He did this on and off for two days. The last time I saw him, I said, "Unless you make it known to me who you are, do not come back. I cannot live this way."

The feeling of being watched was gone.

Our home has an open floor plan. The kitchen, dining room and living room all blend into one space. One day walking from the living room to the kitchen when, off to my right, a head popped up behind the dining room table! It scared me! The head (attached only to a neck, no shoulders or body below) was hovering just above the table. It was an older man, completely bald. He had hundreds of age spots all over his face and head. We looked at each other for a moment, and he was gone.

I credit visits like this to the "candle in the dark" theory. The thinking is, that my gift lights their darkness and they come to see what it is. In the three years since I published my first book, I have learned so much more about paranormal activity. My education on these topics has helped me to understand why and how spirits come into my life.

My life is amazing and I am thankful for it.

Keep in mind that, years earlier I had outlawed spirit from dropping into our bedroom at all hours, I wondered why then this spirit was still lurking in the corner. It has continued to stay in the darkest corner of our room, which is at the foot of the bed, on my side.

I rolled over and was facing away from the area of the spirit. I heard a commotion, a rustling noise. There was nothing alarming about the sound but it got my attention because it was out of place and creepy. I said out loud, "If there is someone or something in our bedroom you had better get the hell out!" I love that my husband does not even comment anymore when things like this happen. He figured I had things under control. Instantly, the room felt lighter, this is always a good sign. I relaxed, fluffed my pillow and settled back to sleep.

I roused out of sleep moments later when I heard the sound of our son coming in through the back door. He was heading to our room, to inform us he was safely home. Just outside our bedroom door, we heard him say, "Damn it, I hate that!" He knocked, came in the room and said, "There is a bright, glowing spirit in the bathroom, floating, by the shower. I love living here!"

I said, "Welcome home, sorry about the spirit. I just kicked the pest out of here and evidently it took harbor in the closest room possible. Interesting, it wasn't glowing when it was in here."

At this point my husband finally spoke up, "Good night to all!"

There was a lingering feeling of spirit energy in the house the next day. I said to the spirit, "Either show yourself or leave. I am done playing with you. It is no longer okay that you are here." The energy in the house calmed down. I take it he left?

Spirit energy levels in the house had been out of control. I could feel it and hear it. My head actually hurt from the high level of energy. I was hearing movement accompanied by walking, the sound of actual footfalls, in the hallway. I do not understand what was happening or why. It had recently been wonderfully serene in the house. From past experiences, I know this type of sudden increase of energy levels, means something has happened or is about to happen. It won't necessarily be something bad but, statistically, it usually is.

I was in the living room, folding laundry, when I heard a snapping sound that originated down the hall. It sounded like the cracking of a whip. I looked in that direction and saw the head and shoulders of a solid black mass. It was above the reclining chair in the living room. A black coat hung on a peg down the hall behind the mass, which made spirit appear

20

as if it had a crown on its head. The mass was there in the hall and then, suddenly, it was gone.

I said out loud, "What the hell was that?" I thought about this for the rest of that day. The cracking sound was similar to a sonic boom, when the sound barrier is broken.

I cannot irrevocable say that this event and the death of my girlfriend from California (who passed just 2 days before) were connected. There were certainly similarities between this jump in spiritual energy and the event of it happening months earlier at the time of my other girlfriend's death.

As I read from my old journals, I realized this dark shadow figure was the same size and color as the one I saw in her home out in California. At the time, I was not sure if it was the spirit of my other girlfriend from back in Michigan or the grandma of my dying girlfriend who was in the bed I sat next to. I do think it was one of them letting me know that this amazing woman would soon be ascending to heaven.

This event did not fit into my paranormal world so was not entered into my journal notes. Thinking about this experience in a different way, I have included it. Life is a journey, this is part of mine.

There is a large Catholic School and University a few miles from my home. In December they display a life size Nativity scene in front of a lovely grotto.

A few years past, my family and I were driving by the nativity scene on the way home from an evening event. I asked my husband to pull in so we could get a closer look.

We walked up the dimly lit path toward the grotto and first came upon the live stock figurines with the three kings. They were atop camels and must have been at least 10 feet tall. Just ahead under the rock grotto, was the Baby Jesus, with Mary and Joseph. They were softly lit by candles only. A gentle snow had started to fall, which punctuated the stillness. The magic was palpable. We approached in silence, looked at the display and then at each other.

Off to the right we noticed there was a small anteroom, filled with the glow of votive prayer candles. My Dad had passed away six months earlier, so I wanted to light a candle for him, to honor him.

The cold Michigan weather kept us from staying longer. We quickly returned to the car and drove home. After peeling off the layers of outerwear, I went to my closet to change into more comfortable clothes. As I bent down to put my slacks in the hamper, a large spider lowered itself from my shoulder to the carpet next to my left foot. I was horrified, screamed and then pounded that spider into the carpet with a shoe! I was creeped out for hours afterward.

My family was not helpful. One of them commented, "Gee just think that thing must have been on you during the entire 20 minute drive home from the Nativity scene."

"Oh man, that spider could have crawled down your sweater!" My husband and son continued on like this for the rest of the night.

I know that we were outside and spiders live there but this was Michigan in December. It was only eight degrees out that night, not exactly spider weather. The candles did throw off heat in the anteroom but it was only a few degrees warmer by the candle stand.

The more I thought about this the more I thought about spiders in general. They seem to show up, time and time again, and have done so over my entire lifetime. As I said, this event is not paranormal, but it is spiritual, and part of the education I am to acquire in this lifetime.

The next morning while thinking about the visit to the grotto, the word "totem" popped into my head. I was not sure I knew the correct definition of a totem so I did some research. It is defined as a "natural object, or animal believed by a particular societies to have spiritual significance." I further learned that certain Native American tribes acknowledge spiders as totems. I continued to research in hopes of discovering the meaning and significance of spider totems.

I found additional information at www.spiritanimal.info/spider-spirit-animal . To quote this website, "The spider is a remarkable figure of feminine energy and creativity in the spirit animal kingdom. Spiders are characterized by the skilled weaving of intricate webs and patience in awaiting their prey. By affinity with the spider spirit animal, you may have qualities of high receptivity and creativity. Having a spider as a power animal or totem helps you tune into life's ebb and flow and ingeniously weave every step of your destiny."

I felt enlightened! This is me! It is how I feel, how I think and what I do. It explained a lot for me and why I have always told people, "I am a spider magnet." I really am. The spider as a spirit animal offers many interpretations, some light and some dark. Interpretation should take into consideration one's own life. As I mentioned earlier, I have had spiders in my life, for all of my life. This new information helped me to understand my life's experiences better. I also acknowledge patience as a key trait I am to acquire in this lifetime.

###

After a long period of restless nights I finally got a good night's sleep in January 2014. I woke up only because my alarm was sounding. It has been many months since I had slept this long and deep, it felt great. I hoped this would continue, sleep keeps me balanced.

Maybe my restful night was a sign. Maybe I was getting a handle on all the death that had been happening around me. I had also, recently, been disturbed by a premonition I had experienced at Christmas time. I knew this was going to be the last Christmas I ever celebrated with both of my parents. One of them would not be alive to celebrate next Christmas.

As I rolled onto my back after that restful sleep, my thousand pound eyelids lifted open. I look at the ceiling over the bed. How long had this thing been watching me while I slept?

This particular morning I saw a grayish black puddle on it. It had a spinning vortex center like water going down a drain. It was spinning with urgency, taking only seconds to disappear up into the ceiling. I laid there for a few more seconds, trying to understand what I just witnessed. Did this really just happen?

It was seriously creepy. What the hell was it? Was it now in my attic? My plan was to check the ceiling over the bed throughout the day. Would I see it during the day too? I was curious but still in denial.

As it turns out I did not have to wait long for an anomaly to occur. Not more than 20 minutes after I got out of bed, I saw a large spider on the ceiling, in the exact spot the vortex had spun up into the attic. I am not a fan of spiders. This one was especially odd though. In the 29 years we have lived in this house, I can count on one hand how many spiders we have had in our bed room. Even more unbelievable, this happened in January... in Michigan. The outside temperature was 25 degrees and over 16 inches of snow had fallen in the last two days. Normally, there would not be a spider in sight for months. This was a mysterious spider.

Of course nature is unpredictable. I probably would not have given this event another thought, it was just a spider. On the other hand, why was it here in January (during the worst winter in Michigan history), and why was it the exact same spot as the vortex? I was intrigued and could not get it out of my head.

I think of spiders as dark, sinister and possibly evil. I looked to the heavens and said, "If I have misinterpreted this event, I am sorry. Just so we are clear, this spot, this area, my home and life are not for the dark or evil but for the light, the good, for God."

I added, "If this was a sign of something good to come, thank you. I will do my best to figure it out. Help from you would be appreciated." After this conversation, I settled down.

I needed an education on vortexes, so I emailed some ghost hunting friends in Kentucky for help. I do not like what I found out. My friend Wes said, "You could actually have created the vortex yourself. Prayer is very effective in closing them. When we sleep our homes are less protected. We tend to let down our defenses without realizing it. I rely on my Spirit Guides and Angels to protect my home when I sleep. Sometime spirits get cocky!"

###

CHAPTER 3

ORBS

I posted a picture of green slime with funky teeth (like in the movie Ghostbusters) on my social network page, Welcome To My Para"Normal" Life. It was captioned, "Orbs are only acceptable evidence of the paranormal if they look like this!" It's cute and funny, but, thank God, it is not true.

I described an event I experienced with orbs in my first book. It was my one and only experience with them up to that point. Since then, I have had two more orb sightings. I was skeptical, prior to my own experiences. Then I saw one, and my dog confirmed it. Yes, I consider her reaction to be valid confirmation. The fact that I ever saw one is shocking, but three, is wild!

These events were all about a year apart, in the same general location. The first orb I saw was the size of a softball. It was gorgeous, Caribbean Sea turquoise. The following two were smaller, about the size of a tennis ball. They glowed brightly, like little suns.

All three orb sightings were in my bedroom, while laying or sitting in bed. The first was directly over the bed, the last two came from the area by the window. One floated over the valance on the window, and the other floated under it.

When I saw the orb that appeared above the valance, the brightly glowing ball floated down five or six inches and simply hovered for about five-seconds. It continued its slow, floating descent, then turned slightly and went up under the valance. Then it was gone. It vanished as quickly as it appeared.

The second time an orb came out from behind the valance, it was from underneath. It was amazingly bright and brighter still since I was seeing it in total darkness. It was like looking straight into the sun. I laid there staring at it, in awe of its pure energy. The glow was coming from the center but had a dimmer outer layer. I remember wishing I was wearing sunglasses so I could look at it in longer increments. It was so bright! I had to rapidly blink while looking at it. This orb seemed smaller than the last one. If it were any bigger, I probably would not have been able to look at it at all. Right before it floated back under the valance, rays of light started to emanate from it. IT WAS AMAZINGLY BEAUTIFUL.

Having the imagination that I do, I knew any second I was going to be shot by one of the rays, and my husband would wake up next to a pile of ashes! Seriously it was a beautiful, little jewel of energy.

It was an honor and a privilege to witness all three orbs.

###

CHAPTER 4

ANGEL VISIT

My husband kissed me good-by as he departed for work. He said, "I am leaving a bit earlier than usual, so I can get home earlier."

A bit of time is my husband's code word for 10 minutes. We call this "Steve time." He honestly has his own clock and way of reading it.

I figured this left me an hour before my alarm would ring. It was cozy with Lola tucked close to me. She was snoring. I quickly joined her in sleep.

When I awoke, it seemed I had just fallen asleep seconds earlier. My eyes flutter, and I noticed movement in the room. It was a shape of a person, entering my bedroom. The figure came around the end of the bed, and I lost sight of it. I felt the bed compress down just behind me. The feeling faded as I became more awake.

I could not tell whether it was male or female. The spirit was in a white gown, with a braided cord tied at the waist. It looked more angelic than any spirits I have ever seen.

I ask for angel protection every night while we sleep. Was this my Angel protection or my ever present Spirit Guide?

###

This event, and the one to follow, holds immense power and grace. It will stay in my heart and memory for the rest of my life.

It was a week day morning, like any other. I was just waking up but still between the two states of being. I was lying on my back. I reached over to my right to see if Lola was still in bed with me. I did not feel her so I turned to look. My attention was immediately drawn in the direction of the closet.

There was a tiny speck of intense, gold light floating toward the bed. As the light got closer, it exponentially increased in size and took on the shape of a person. This was more than a spirit or ghost. It was glowing, unlike any spirit I have ever seen. It was wearing a beautiful gown of deep purple and rich, gold tones. The form became the height of an above average human. It stopped its approach just short of colliding with the side of the bed. Still glowing but now with rays shooting out, just like the sun. I realized this vision was an angel, a special angel. I was in the presence of undeniable peace, beauty and grace. It was the most amazing thing I have ever witnessed.

As the Angel floated next to the bed, in my mind I hear, "All will be well."

"Excuse me?"

Again, in my mind, I hear, "All will be well."

Evidentially, its purpose was to speak those words to me because as soon as I heard them, the angel started to retreat backward toward the closet. I was completely mesmerized as I watched it shrink back into the tiny, bright light. And then it was gone.

I gulping for air, apparently I had been holding my breath. I was confused, but knew at some point, this visit would make sense.

It was a wonderful and wondrous time in life for our family. Our son was about to graduate from high school and head off to college in the fall. An accomplishment he had earned and a step he was ready to take.

We hosted his graduation party in early June. He was one of the first parties of the season. My intuition told me it was the right date to choose. Unbeknownst to me, there was a reason it was supposed to be that day. The reason would soon be revealed.

The day after his graduation party, we were exhausted. All that planning and emotional excitement wore us out. My husband and I were resting in the living room when our son came to tell us he was heading over to his friends graduation party.

Our son moved and stood directly in front of me and said, "I need a doctor's appointment. I found a lump. It's on the back of my left testicle. I think it is probably just a varicose vein from sports, but I feel I should have it checked. I want to be sure."

I said, "Of course you should." Since it was Sunday, I

continued, "We can call tomorrow morning to set something up."

I encourage him to make the call himself since he was about to begin his adult life and be out on his own.

The next morning he was up and on the phone right away. I should have red flagged that action, because he usually sleeps in, whenever he can. The appointment was set for two weeks out. Apparently the doctor was going on vacation so that was the earliest appointment available. My son and I agreed that would be fine, there was no rush.

I headed for the shower, and within 5 minutes, a voice in my head screamed, "Move the appointment." I hurried out of the shower, got dressed and thought of ways to say to my son that I was stepping in to call the doctor. I did not want to offend him or his abilities but knew I needed to get him an earlier appointment. There is a fine line here, he needs to know he is his own person, but my gut was roaring at me to step in. I also did not want to alarm him.

I walked to his room and said, "Hey would you mind if I called the doctor's office to see if maybe I can swing an earlier appointment for you? You seemed to want an earlier date."

He said, "I do not mind Mom, not at all."

"Okay, as long as I'm not stepping on your toes here."

He understood. I was relieved. I calling the doctor's office, used every trick in the book and finally got them to squeeze in an appointment for him at the end of the week, on Friday.

On appointment day, the doctor checked him over and, to

my surprise asked me join them in the exam room after my son got dressed. I sat down in a chair next to the exam table where my son was sitting. The doctor said, "Well this could be several things, a varicose vein, an injury or cancer."

My head was spinning after hearing the "C" word. That had never crossed my mind. After a moment, denial kicked in. I KNEW it was just a varicose vein, so, no problem.

The doctor excused himself, was gone for a few minutes and came back in with an appointment card. He gave it to my son. He scheduled an ultrasound for him the next morning. Again, I thought, no problem, better safe than sorry.

The ultrasound was done the next morning. Our son had been home only an hour after his appointment when the phone rang. It was the doctor; he had made an appointment for him to see a Urologist on Monday. It was cancer.

Life stopped.... I went numb.

As far as the urologist could tell, the testicular cancer was Stage 1. My husband, our son and I stood at the nurse's desk as they set the surgery date for that coming Thursday.

Thankfully the surgery went great. It was outpatient, we went home within hours. My husband and I held on to each other while we watched our son sleep.

He stared his first round of chemotherapy the third week of August. His last day of chemo was his first day of college. I picked him up after his first class ended at 8 am. It was a two hour drive to get him, and two more hours back to the hospital. He had his treatment and then his dad got him back to school. He had a night class that first day of college and attended that as well. That must have been a long, terrifying day for our son.

His first year of college flew by, and his test results showed he was still cancer free! He will not be considered permanently cancer free for ten years. A dream that at the moment seems so far off.

After those encouraging test results arrived in the mail, we hugged, we cried, we thanked God and our son went off to celebrate with his girlfriend. I was alone in the house, thinking about this hell of a firestorm we had come through. A memory hit me.

"All will be well"

I stood up and started to cry. Tears were streaming down my face. I spoke out loud and said, "You are so thick Exie Susanne! This is why the angel spoke to you. It was meant to help you, to keep your mind from fracturing."

I have to admit, I nearly lost my mind during that year. It was almost more than I could handle. I now know how strong I can be. Speaking to the angel, I said, "Thank you, thank you, thank you." I know the angel visit was to help bring me peace and it finally did, a year later.

I began researching angels because I wanted a better explanation of what I saw that day. There were several things I discovered that stuck me. Not the least being, that I was visited in the first place. The most striking aspect of my angel visit was the vibrant colors and the 3D nature of my vision. It was as if a living person was standing right in front of me.

When I researched the angel's specific purple and gold

colored clothing, draped in a Romanesque style, I discovered something amazing. I had been visited by the Arch Angle Saint Michael. He is the warrior. I found this fitting. Our son was battling for his life. My husband and I were battling for our sanity.

I could not be more thankful for this message and gift of love from Saint Michael.

###

CHAPTER 5

LOSS

In the dedications section of my first book, I included a girlfriend of mine and thanked her for being in my life. Most of all, I am thankful for her understand and nonjudgmental nature. We were weird little kids!

Sadly, before my book came out and could read it, she became ill and was diagnosed with lung cancer. I was never told what stage of cancer she had at the time of diagnoses, so I did not know how much time she had to live. I quickly realized though, that her intense, initial treatments meant the cancer was advanced.

The last time I saw her was early fall and I knew then, I would never see her alive again.

I tried to visit her on many occasions but her family needed time with her and her health deteriorated quickly. I finally called her home and told the person that answered, "I am coming over, Wednesday at 11 a.m." I was told that would be fine.

I woke up the day of the much anticipated visit only to feel like it was not to be. Sure enough, the phone rang mid-morning, and I said to my husband, "Here we go."

It was one of my friend's sisters calling to tell me that she had passed away. I already knew.

I laughed and cried at the same time as I said to my husband, "I have had people go to great lengths not to see me, but this one takes the cake." I feel into my husband's open arms and sobbed.

Days went by and my friend's spirit had not come to visit me. I was deeply saddened and confused. Oddly, I started seeing shadow movement around the house. It was about the size of a cat. I was heating a cup of coffee in the microwave when I first noticed the reflection of a small animal sitting on the back of the couch. It appeared to be looking out the window.

When the shadow shifted a bit so did my opinion. It was not a cat, it was a small dog. The same size and shape of my girlfriend's dog. When I saw him it brought to mind something she told me. The last time I saw her, she said, "I would like to see the lake one more time, it is so beautiful." We tried to make that happen, but physically she was not strong enough.

My friend was laid to rest the following Monday. Four days later, I stepped out of my bedroom and into the hall, there she was! Two poster board size photos, head and shoulders only, appeared of her. They were floating in midair, one diagonally above the other. They were bright smiling reminders of the friend I love and will miss.

The photos were beautifully ornate, hand carved wood frames. They appeared to be antique. She loved antiques. The fact that drama permeated this entire event was perfect. She loved that as well!

As these framed photos moved diagonally down toward me, her face seemed to get brighter. It was like they were backlit. As each reached eye level, they started to fade and were gone by the time they moved past me.

What crossed my mind first after the photos disappeared was it seemed these were merely a representation of her. That she wanted me to know she was thinking of me but busy and would catch up with me later.

Her oldest son and his wife were expecting a baby. They asked me if the baby could be her coming back, reincarnation. I told them, "You never know!" My teachings do not lean in that direction, it would be too soon for her to do so. There are other teachings that do not agree with me, so I suggest they draw their own conclusion after the baby's birth. Who am I to break already broken hearts?

God Bless dear friend, see you on the other side. Cheers!

As we were literally heading out the door to the funeral home for the girlfriend I just talked about, the phone rang. Looking at the read out on my cell phone, I saw the incoming number and my stomach knotted up. Emotional over load was about to head into atom bomb proportions.

The number calling was that of my other lifelong girlfriend living in southern California. She was battling breast cancer. I knew it was not going to be her on the phone but God how I wanted it to be. Unfortunately, I was right it was her husband. "Hello" was all I could get out.

He said, "You need to come out here as soon as you can, if you want to see her." His voice broke, so did my heart. My two oldest and dearest friends were leaving me here alone.

I said, "Okay. I will get a flight out in a day or two. I will call you in the morning with flight info. I am so sorry."

He said, "I'm sorry to call on such short notice but the doctor only told us today that the drugs to fight this monster are no longer working, she has less than two months." He had no more voice to continue.

I needed to leave for the funeral but no way was I hanging up on this man. I said, "When is good time for me to come out and see her?" He immediately gave me a date, knowing I would drop everything and be there.

I arrived in San Diego, California two weeks later, his date choice. There had been family staying in the house, and helping him care for her. They left the day before I arrived.

I felt submerged in water as I struggled to walk through their home. It was emotional just to be there. I reached the side of her hospital bed, which was set up in the middle of the bright living room. She turned and looked at me. She had not been told I was coming. I smiled brightly into the shocked face of my embattled hero.

We embraced and wept. She whispered into my ear, "Oh Sue B, it got me. It wasn't supposed to get me."

"Oh my dearest friend, I am more shocked by this turn of events than I can say. This is not what was supposed to happen. Shit."

She chuckled at my expletive and that made me smile. We eventually let go of our hug, but I stayed seated on the side of the bed. We talked until she got tired and feel asleep. I went to the guest suite to unpack.

I have had many difficult challenges put in my path, but this was at the top of the list. I watching as my brilliant, accomplished lifelong friend die. Good God I wanted my husband with me. I needed his support. I did not feel I had the strength to do this without him.

Several hours later, she and I visited a bit more. She again needed rest. I was seated on the couch by her bedside, reading, and listening to the stereo. I felt the energy in the room change. I looked up from my book to acknowledge the person that had just entered the room. Standing there was a full shadow person. It was on the other side of her bed, looking at me. The shadow moved to the foot of the hospital bed, looked at my girlfriend and faded away.

As the spirit shadow faded, I realized the song on the radio had significance to the recent passing of my other girlfriend. This song had been playing on the radio at home when I got the official phone call that my other girlfriend had passed away. The music told me who the spirit shadow was.

A short time later I spotted more shadow movement; this time to my far right. It moved on the other side of the desk chair. The shadow looked blurred as it moved past the ventilated holes in the chairs fabric. A cool effect actually!

I will admit I thought this might be my girlfriend again, but I was not so sure. It felt different. A conversation I would have the next day, would give me the answers.

Many exhausting hours later, it was time to turn in. I was in the guest room trying to get a grip on this whole situation, her sickness and the future without her. I was so sad. I could feel spirit energies all day as I sat in the room with my girlfriend. Now in the guest room, I felt a presence and knew I was no longer alone in the room. Off to the right, in the area of the bathroom sink, a shadow appeared. Slowly becoming visible right before my eyes. It was nice and subtle, not aggressive or frightening.

Questions popped into my head for this spirit. "Why are you here?" I thought there might be question as to my presence, so I said, "I am a long time friend of hers. I love and care about her as a sister. I was invited by her husband. I am here to say good-bye, and help anyway I can. I am told time is very short, is that correct?"

No answer came from my last question, I assumed because the spirit sensed I already knew that answer. I turned out the light, but the shadow person stayed and watched me as I slept. It was comforting. I took it as a show of support for the entire household. I hoped like hell it was!

I stumbled into the shower early the next morning, the hot water felt grand. I glanced up and out the double frost glass shower doors. I watched a shadow move all the way across the room and out the far wall. The message in my head told me to get moving!

After breakfast, my girlfriend and her daughter were together by the bed and I decided to bring all this shadow movement I had been seeing. Much to my surprise neither of them was shocked by what I said. In fact they both said, "It's Nana." This is my girlfriend's grandmother. They were very close and had a tight bond. She was a sweet, giving person. I had actually met her many years earlier.

My girlfriend continued, "Someone has been standing on the right side my bed, next to the head. I see them there a lot" It makes sense that it would be her loving Nana, guarding over her, ready to escort her granddaughter home when it is her time.

I did not see any more shadow movement after that morning. I felt it was a sign of acceptance and support to me on that first extremely tough day. I am thankful.

I flew back to Detroit the next morning. I was exhausted, gutted by sadness. I prayed the seat next to me would remain empty. They announced the flight was totally full, I did not hold out much hope as passenger after passenger walked up to my row. As the plane backed away from the terminal, I smiled toward heaven and said thank you. Next to me were two empty seats! They were the only ones on the entire plane. When allowed, I stretched out, put my jacket under my head and slept.

The loss of friend is difficult. The loss of two friends at nearly the same time was unbearable.

As for the Sue B nick name. Back in the sixth grade my girlfriend nicknamed me that. My middle name is Susanne, so short for that, Sue. My maiden name is Bruce, thus the B. I shall miss hearing her call me that, it was special.

The loss of a friend of this magnitude is painful and will be felt for many years to come. Rest in peace.

###

A long time friend of the family called with heart breaking news. Her husband had passed away. She called to personally let us know, but also to see if I had heard anything from him. I had not gotten a message nor had I felt any new spirits around me. That was the last thing in the world I wanted to say to her but it was the truth. Her voice was full of hope that I had heard from him.

I said, "I am sorry that I have not gotten any messages. I will try to contact him. If I get something, I will call you." We hung up. I was shocked, sad for her and the kids. I put the phone down, and started a conversation out loud to the heavens. "My friend, I am so sorry to hear you have left this Earthly plane and your loving family."

At this point, I was standing in the laundry room. I pace when I talk. I was still conversing with him and doing laundry. When I bent back up from the dryer the light on the laundry room ceiling went out. Click! Not batting and eye, I said, "Are you in heaven, did you ascend and are you okay?"

I did not get a direct answer, but I knew in my gut that he had and was fine. I smiled, and replied, "Thank you, it is nice to hear from you."

The light came back on. Click.

With laundry in tow, I went back to the living room. I had a feeling that I needed to speak with my Spirit Guide, if I could. "Hello Spirit Guide. Do you know anything about the husband of my friend that just passed away?" In my head I heard, "Hello Susanne. He has arisen. He has come back down and is presently at the house with them."

Humbly I said, "Thank you."

The reply, "You are welcome Susanne."

I felt good about this, confident in the message. I knew I had not made this up in my head. Arisen is not in my every-day vocabulary. Later in the day, I called my friend back to let her know what I had been told by her husband and by my Spirit Guide. She said, "I know he has been at the house, I can feel him."

When I visited the funeral home, I could feel him in the room, checking out the vast number of people that had come to pay respects.

The tide is changing. I am opening up. My belief is filling the void of uncertainty. I am thankful to be able to offer help and comfort.

###

CHAPTER 6

VISITS IN DREAMS AND MESSAGES IN MU-SIC

This is a reiteration of another event described in the book. I bring it back up because it holds the message I received from my girlfriends, the lesson I learned and closure to their deaths. I lost two lifelong girlfriends, in the span of three months, both to cancer.

My girlfriend had moved back to California years ago. She was born and lived there until sixth grade, when her family moved here to Michigan. After she graduated from Michigan State University, she moved back to her beloved California. We lost touch with each other, except for birthdays and holidays.

We rarely communicate via the computer. She was a traditionalist and loved getting mail delivered to the house. I, being a tech loving nerd, am just the opposite. When her diagnoses of breast cancer came, I relented and mailed at least one lighthearted letter a week. Once a month I would mail a gift. A handmade teddy bear, body lotions, anything to make her feel a bit pampered. We were also using email and talking on the phone often. Through all this communication, we discovered that life had indeed moved on, but we learned just how much our lives had paralleled the same road. We were close again; it felt as if no time had passed. It had been thirty years.

After she passed, I was so lonely. It hit me hard. I had lost another person that I totally trusted. She was supposed to beat this killing machine called cancer! I believed she could beat it.

While staring at the ceiling, I asked my girlfriend, "Why have you not come to see me? I want to know that you are okay and that you have gone home to Heaven. Please find a way to let me know. Thank you." I knew she was fine but was pouting and feeling sorry for myself.

Within the week, she came to me in a dream. Just like a photo bomb, she popped in! It was just her face; she was looking me directly in the eyes. She was serious. She did not verbalize with spoken words but I still heard her say, "Here I am, notice me. Yes, this is real and what you asked me to do."

She looked great, healed and healthy. However, I felt she had something else on her mind, a question for me. When that thought crossed my mind my clock radio/alarm went off and the song that played was the same one I had heard at her home. As she lay in the hospital bed, this song came on the stereo as shadows of spirit moved about the room.

To paraphrase the song: "I have died everyday waiting for you." This was her question, "Why did you not come to see me sooner?" I had tried, repeatedly with both my girlfriends.

I have the same answer for both of my girlfriends who played this song for me. Both of these women had loving, amazing people, caregivers watching over them. At the same time these caregivers were being diligent, they inadvertently kept people away. Was that what happened here, from my point of view, yes. As hurt as I was at the time, I said to my husband, "Everything happens the way it is supposed to."

My closure came in the form of a dream, for both of them. They were smiling, happy, healthy and each told me they were fine. They said everything was great. That they would come check on me and I would know when they were around. They said they would greet me when it was my time to go home to heaven. That freaked me out a little, but they both said it was going to many years yet. I was relieved!

The dreams were great, important to me, because I needed closure. I also needed to know, for my one girlfriend, that she had gone home to Heaven. I was worried she might have preferred to stay with her husband and daughter. She goes to them a great deal but she is not earth bound. She is free. Both of my friends are free.

I dream in vivid color and full of action. This is how my mind works out situations and problems, while my body rests. This dream made me sit straight up in bed when it was over.

I'm in my childhood bedroom, going through everything hanging in my closet. I was working hard, trying to put an outfit together for the day. It was not going well. In my peripheral view, I saw my Aunt Exie. She went by in the hallway outside my room. She did nothing else but stared straight ahead and robotically walk past my door from right to left. She did this twice.

It was disturbing and woke me up. I was disturbed because the people in my dreams who acted this way were usually dead. My aunt was not dead. Denial seeped in. I had thought of her earlier that day, so maybe that is why she was in my dream. I went back to sleep. Four days after this dream, my Aunt had a massive stroke and passed away five days later.

My cousin had placed her mom, my aunt, in a beautifully caring hospice center. My family and I went to say good-bye. It was so difficult, but it was something we wanted to do. She was in a comma, but all believed she knew we were there. My son took his girlfriend to introduce them to each other. My husband and I left the three of them alone as my son spoke in hushed tones to his great aunt and with his amazing girlfriend by his side.

The next morning at 6:12 a.m., I was awakened by my Aunt saying good bye to me. I said, "Good-bye Aunt Exie, I love you. Thank you for coming to see me. I am glad you let go and are going home to God, family and friends."

I got out of bed because I knew the phone was going to ring soon. Someone would be calling to inform us of her passing. I wanted some coffee before the call came.

After I talked with my cousin, I thought about the passing of another wonderful family member. She had gone home to God. That left me to be the only "Exie" in the family.

I woke up feeling a bit stymied because of the dream I just experienced. I was standing on the edge of a huge expanse lawn. It was the perfect shade of green. It made me thing of

The Hampton's. I knew in my gut there was a huge mansion, directly behind me, even without turning around. That house did not matter because my heart was focus out over the beautiful lawn, toward a different home off in the distance.

There seemed to be a celebration going on, a large gathering. I was not sure of the occasion, but I wanted to attend. I felt my feet come off the ground. I floated up and forward, toward the gathering at the distant mansion. The grass was very tall but did not hinder my progress. I flew by the trees; they seemed to make a path.

When I arrived I was welcomed. It was a place of peace. I felt completely relaxed and utterly happy. The thought of my grandfather (on my mom's side of the family) came to mind. With that thought, I became driven to see him. I thought he would be attending this function. Before I could enter the mansion, several people I did not know floated up to me asking me questions about the house. I told them they could not enter, but I could. I did add, after being short with them, "It is not your time yet, you may not enter."

The house was in the shaker style. It looked old outside but was totally modernized on the inside. All across the bottom of the house were double doors, thrown open welcomingly. I stood there taking it all in, not sure what to do next. I turned when I felt a presence behind me. Presence was the perfect word, they were not solid like you and I. The spirit floated in through one of the sets of doors, and beckoned me to follow.

We entered a room that was beautifully decorated; it appeared to be a greeting area. The walls were finished with panels of wood that gleamed from being polished. There were people in the area some seated, others standing. They were all in conversation with one another. I was looking at them to see if I knew anyone. I spotted an uncle of mine who had passed away many years earlier. I asked him, "Have you seen my Grandma?"

He said, "Try the next room." His lips had not moved but I heard him just the same.

On my left there was an archway, the room on the other side glowed. I had to see it. I floated into the room. It was the kitchen, all in bright white. There were two people busily moving about but neither was my grandmother, so I moved to the next room. As I passed them, they acknowledge my presence with a polite nod and went back about their duties. As I floated around the kitchen island, I caught sight of the next room, the dining room. There was a long sold wood table and at the head was my Grandmother.

As I floated into the room, simply wishing to say hello, I got the feeling this was not a good time. However when I looked at the people seated around the table, they stopped their conversations, looked from me to my Grandma at the head of the table. They smiled at her and then me, a knowing smile of a special moment. I was relieved to feel they did not mind that I was there.

Insecurity was taking over, as I was leaving, I looked to a person seated behind me, seeking to get permission to stay. It was my aunt. Even in my dream state I knew she should not be here either, she was also still alive. I asked her, "Is it okay for me to approach my Grandma?"

She laughed, motioned with her hand, and said, "Go ahead!"

When I reached my grandma, we hugged. I asked her, "Where is Grandpa?"

She said, "I'm very sorry child, he was not able to be here today."

We hugged each other a last time, it felt warm and I felt her love for me. The strong feeling brought tears.

She said, "Poor child."

As I came jarringly awake, I realized I was hearing tapping. The tapping was coming from the hall, on my bedroom door-frame. I had a doctor's appointment in 45 minutes, and my alarm was not set.

Was I actually with my family in some far off place? Was I really floating in the grass? Was I traveling through a mansion? I cannot say with certainty that I was, no. I do bring this dream up when there is discussion of what is called "astral projection". It is described as an "out of body" experience. Because this was my dream and cannot be proven, I use it as an example. It provided me with insights to my problems and the strength my grandmother always had in life. It gave me a question as well, what was my aunt doing there?

###

My husband and I went on a short vacation to the gulf coast of Florida. It felt nice to bask in the sun on gorgeous, white sand beaches. Just before going to sleep one night, he said, "Tomorrow we are half way through our time here, why does it go so fast!"

That night I had an extremely vivid dream. Once I was fully awake, I hoped it was truly only a dream. I had dreamt of death. In the first part of the dream, this person was my older brother but as the dream progressed, this person's image became blurred and the face became someone else. It became the face of a friend's father.

As the facial change was happening, a bright yellow, glowing light came over his face. As the facial features became more distinct, the glow lessened from the face area and moved to around his head. It made me think of a halo. A second person appeared behind him to his right; I was not sure who this was.

Even with the facial change, I was still leaning toward this person being my brother. I was a mess with that though for about an hour after I woke up. I was bad company for breakfast, I could not think of anything else. When my husband asked me, for the third time, "What is wrong?"
I finally told him, "I had a dream about someone dying. I think it might be," I stopped talking. "No, I'm wrong, it was not my brother. It is our neighbor's father."

"Holy shit, what makes you say this?" He was rightfully concerned.

"I dreamt it, but the details were too real not to have actually happened."

I grabbed my cell phone and hit the home button. Our family would not call and interrupt vacation, especially with it almost over, so I called them. They did not have any news for us of any kind. That was good, I actually started to breathe again and contemplated another day at the beach.

I decided to do a quick check of my social media page before heading out to the beach. One post down on the page and there was the first RIP post. It was referring to our friend's father. I told my husband and together we composed a private message to our friends and their families.

I have never foreshadowed a death, it shook me up. Moreover I was upset because of the great, kind and funny man we had all lost. RIP kind Sir.

Not all of my insights and premonitions come in a dream.

It is Christmas and I am sick, extremely sick, with head and chest congestion. I was mad because I love Christmas and entertaining this time of year. Christmas morning was awful and I could hardly get myself out of bed. My parents were due to arrive about 1:30 p.m. to exchange gifts, have appetizers, sip some wine and share some time together as family. I had planned a huge prime rib dinner. This has always been my favorite day of the year. I knew in my gut it would be the last exactly like it, and I there was, bed ridden.

My son and husband came into the bedroom to check on me, I was crying. My husband said, "Relax, there is always next year!"

I looked at them and said, "No, this will be the last like it, with all of us. One of my parents will not make it to next Christmas. One of them will no longer be in this physical world by then. I am so sad and mad." I knew my husband and son did not believe me. I did not want to believe me.

Sadly, the next summer my father passed away from complications of heart surgery.

###

CHAPTER 7

HELPING, HEARING AND COUNSELING

Death does not work on our schedule. I flew home from saying good-bye to my lifelong girlfriend in California in time to do laundry, repack and head up north. In Michigan, we refer to up state as "up north." In this case, I was heading to an area called Traverse City for a book signing. It was beautiful up there on the bay.

Thankfully, my husband joined me for this trip. I was able to get some sleep as we made the four hour drive.

I arrived at the bookstore, set at my table with a pen in my hand. I was ready to sign and sell my book. I always feel a bit nervous at book signings. It takes me about ten minutes to settle down. I swear the patrons feel this because the minute my stomach is relaxed, people start coming by the table.

The first to do so was a tall gentleman in his early seventies. He had kind eyes and a tight smile. He opened the conversation with his name and a confession. "I believe this stuff," was all he said, followed by another tight-lipped smile. He stole my heart. I smiled in return, but knew he was hurting and missing someone.

Before I could say anything, he said, "I lost my wife a year ago Thanksgiving time to cancer. She comes to see me in the garden. I know because she places a hand on my shoulder."

I sat quiet for a moment, feeling honored that he had shared this treasured information with me. Stalling for a moment and fighting back tears. I scooting forward in my chair, to get closer to him, and I asked, "Do you talk to her? You can, you know."

"I do," he said. "I tell her I'm glad she is here with me."

My eyes were brimming with tears, and I said, "That is beautiful. She is checking on you and knows right where to find you!"

He said, "I want your book."

"I would love that, thank you," was all I could squeeze out.

After I signed the book, I stood to hand it to him. We looked into each other eyes. I said, "Thank you for sharing your private story with me."

He said, "No, thank you!"

After he went to the counter and paid for the book, he came back by my table to say good-bye. I watched as he walked away. He left the store and went out onto the crowed sidewalk. He then disappeared from my sight. My thoughts of this gentle man were kindly interrupted, by a bookstore employee. I had not realized she was standing there, and had witnessed the entire transaction. When I looked at her, she had watery eyes, and so did I. "Oh my," was all she could manage.

I said, "This happens quite a lot. I am emotionally tired after I do a signing."

She said, "You did a beautiful thing there."

"Thank you, but he did all the work. All I did was listen."

She said, "You were probably his only communication for the day, you did a beautiful thing."

She walked away; I grabbed a tissue and dried my eyes. I had only been in the chair for twenty minutes. I still had an hour and forty minutes to go! "Lord, give me strength."

After this exchange, there was a continual flow of store customers who came up to my table. I chatted with many people that day. They talked of paranormal events they had experienced. I signed books and enjoyed their fantastic stories.

My husband, who had been wandering the bookstore, appeared by my side. I turning to talk with him, but he suddenly stopped talking and was looking behind me. I turned to face the front of the table. I did not expect what I saw standing in front of me. It was a young girl, a wisp of a girl, pale and stormy looking. She had stringy long white blond hair, pale skin and dark circles under her eyes. The fact she was dressed in all black made the entire effect perfect. As I studied her more, I noticed a glow that came from deep inside her. She was a beautiful child.

I said, "Hi!"

Very seriously, she asked, "Do you see dead things?"

"Yes," I said.

She said, "So do I!"

I already knew that answer by her presence and the way she was looking at me.

I then asked, "How old are you?"

"I am eleven. I go to school, well for now at another building, ours is being fixed. It's in a very old school. There is a little girl there."

I assumed she meant a dead little girl and asked, "Is that okay?"

"Yes," she said, "Its fine. She is nice and likes us."

I said, "You do know that if she comes around during a time you need to doing school work, you can send her away?"

She said, "No, it's okay, she is nice."

I said, "I am glad."

Finally breaking eye contact with each other. She looked down at my book, then back up at me. "I have to go."

As she turned to go, I thanked her for stopping to talk to me. She looked back at me, blank-faced and walked away. I badly wanted to see her parents, but never did.

I was left feeling rather stupid, inept and eons behind her in lessons on life. I know she is the oldest living soul I have ever encountered.

When my husband came back to the table, I realized I was holding my hand over my heart. I felt as if she had been in there and touched me to my soul. Later that evening, I wondered if she and I might have talked longer if I had more experience with my gift. I got the feeling from her that she was wasting her time because she knew more than me. She felt superior to me in knowledge.

I concluded that it does not matter what she thinks or knows. What matters to me is my own personal growth. I judged her and assumed she knew less than me regarding paranormal matters because of her age. This was a mistake.

I know she has things to work on in her lifetime, as we all do. My conclusion, who knows for sure, in such a short snippet of time with a person, what they really know or think. We can only know, for sure, what is in our own hearts and minds.

It was nice meeting her. I learned a lot from her but will admit she left me with a creepy feeling.

This event will appear here as if it happened all in one day. In actuality, it was a six day chain of events. This happens to me some times because I choose to ignore what I have been feeling and picking up, spiritually.

Days before I felt this spirit, I foolishly made the statement, "The spirits don't seem to be around me anymore." Then when I did feel something, I thought possibly I was forcing the issue because I missed the feeling.

This event was more than just a feeling, I was seeing

shadows move and the full outline of a shadow person in dark corners of certain rooms. Once these things repeated themselves over the course of several days, I settled myself and felt the energy I had been ignoring.

I checked my email and saw one that said, "Death Notice." It came from someone I did not know, so I almost deleted. I was curious, so I open it. It got even weirder. The note was informing me of the death of a person I had never met but talked to many times. The notice was a not surprising to me. Earlier that week I thought about her and knew something was wrong.

The person who sent the touching email was a best friend of the woman that passed. My connection to the deceased was our sons, and a cancer support organization. At the time, I was a counselor for the organization. My son introduced me to this organization during his cancer battle. He is a six-year survivor and counting! Thank you God. She and I were caregivers for our sons. We talked only over the phone.

At the time of her son's passing, my son was just over a year cancer free, so my memory of it all was very fresh. Her son lived out of state, which was difficult. This young man had stomach cancer. There is no cure for this type of cancer and the treatments they had tried did not work. We did not discuss how far along his cancer was, she did not want to talk about it. He sadly lost his battle within the year of our meeting and talking.

She called one day, and I was pleased to hear from her. However, once the conversation started I knew what she was going to say was not going to be good. This charming and brilliant woman delivered the news about her sons passing in a stoic and calm manor. She impressed and humbled me. I was not prepared for the news of his death. It was devastated to hear. We talked for a little while and then hung up. I sat with a strangle hold on the phone and cried for both mother and son.

The night before she called, I had a spirit visitation. It was an unfamiliar, male spirit. He wanted something but I did could not figure out what it was.

I gathered enough courage during my phone conversation to tell her about the male spirit visitation the night before. I asked her to describe her son. His hair color, skin color, etc. Without a picture of him I could not be sure it was him.

Was this a coincidence? By now you know how I feel about those!

I felt bad about possibly freaking her out. Mental note, timing is everything. I remember just before we hung up, she said, "I will be in touch." I knew in my gut, we would never talk again…we never did. I did not know that it would be because of her death.

It is a very sad situation. I guess her son's passing was a final straw for her. In my mind, this passing, her journey home was very much underway long before she died. I hope to never understand this in my own life.

God bless this amazing woman and loving mom. It was truly an honor to have met, and learn from you. Thank you.

###

CHAPTER 8

BEING FOLLOWED BY SPIRITS AND GHOSTS

My father needed a small procedure before he could have surgery to repair a heart valve. At the hospital, on the day of the procedure, we took a dedicated elevator from the heart center's waiting room to the second floor.

Hours later, the procedure was successfully completed and told we could take my Dad home. Mom and a nurse were getting Dad ready to go, so I was sent to retrieve the car and bring it to the main doors.

I stepped off the elevator and into the heart center's waiting area. I glanced up over the now mostly vacant seating area, and noticed something out of place. In the center of the room was a woman sitting perfectly straight in a chair. I could see her but I could also see through her. She was wearing a brown suit, skirt and blazer, with a white blouse that had a matching fabric tie at the neck. It was out of style by twenty-five years. Her brown hair, pulled tightly back into a bun at the base of her neck. Posture was perfect and her hands were neatly folded in her lap. She had a very pleasant look on her pretty face.

When I was about half way across the waiting room, I looked back at her. She was looking directly at me, watching my progress across the room. I brought my attention back to the walkway for a split second. When I looked back, she was gone!

I stopping immediately and looked back toward the reception desk. The woman sitting at the desk was the spitting image of the spirit I just saw. I continued walking. I could not help but wonder if the receptionist knew she has a family member that comes to work with her. This was such a touching and sweet event.

We have a renowned art museum called "The Detroit Institute of Arts." It is more than exhibits. They also have film theaters, lecture facilities and studios for art instruction.

My particular favorite thing they do is showcase amazing, special exhibits. The one I attended on this day featured Rembrandt's works. I admire his talent and his mind. I attended with a friend of mine who I consider brilliant and wonderfully diverse. She too admires this artist.

Thoroughly entranced by all that surrounded me I lost track of my friend and everyone else attending the exhibit. As I stood in front of his work "Faces of Jesus," there was a heavy breath in my left ear. It was followed by four or five indistinguishable words. I quickly looked up from the painting and around the room in every direction. My friend and I were the only ones in the room. She asked me, "What's with the look? Are you okay?"

"No, and yes I just had someone exhale heavily by my left ear, then say something but I could not understand. Did you hear it, too?"

She smiled, "No, I did not hear it. Do you have any idea how special you are?"

I replied, "Let's not get carried away here. I want to check out the acoustics before I even slightly consider this paranormal."

I know places like this can have weird acoustics, so I had my friend move all around the room. I asked her to exhale loudly and then say four or five words. It quickly became a laughing matter once she and I started using interesting unrepeatable words. The experiment was over.

I could not draw a conclusion about this event. We could not replicate it. All I know is that it was an odd sensation.

My husband and I traveled to Lexington, Kentucky. I had been invited to the Mystical Paranormal Fair, to sign, sell my book and to speak at the fair. My husband, bless his heart, was driving me down to the event. It was only a six hour drive.

We arrived late in the afternoon, the day before the event, to set up. They had a table for me at one end of the building. Just beyond where I was setting up, the building was used as an art and photo studio. The person that greeted us said to help ourselves to a tour around the place, and let the staff know if we needed anything. I did not say anything to my husband at the time, but I knew we were not touring the building alone. I felt followed and watched the entire time I was in that building.

The next morning, we finished setting up and I went to a group participants meeting. The meeting was run by Patti

Starr, the event organizer. Introductions were made by all and a blessing given. The talent (psychics, healer and the like) were giving off a huge amount of energy during the blessing. I was giving off energy, too, but of the nervous kind. The woman next to me could feel it and told me relax, it was going to be great. I appreciated that!

Back at my table, Patti's husband (and co-organizer of the event) Chuck Starr, came over and introduced himself. We chatted for a while about ghosts. Chuck asked me, "Can you feel or see our ghost here?"

I laughed, "As a matter of fact, I felt him yesterday as we walked around the place. I think it is a male spirit." This line of conversation helped me relax. The show was about to begin and I was ready

Maybe twenty minutes after the show started, I saw a few shadows moving in the back room, past where I was set up. I felt it was their ghost and hoped he would show up better for me eventually. Later that afternoon, in the lunch room area of the building getting coffee, and I saw the shadow again. I saw him move past a sidelight of the door into the art gallery. He, evidently, liked to move around a lot.

Those were the most remarkable events I had with their ghost that weekend. I sensed him all over the place as I moved around the building. I had the feeling he was checking me out since I was the new girl!

The fair was set up differently then I had ever seen before. There were two main halls. Down each hall, on either side, there were rooms for the gifted people to do their work. This particular weekend there were healers, a shaman, card readers, crystal healers and a pet psychic.

Everyone was kind, southern hospitality is a real thing. One of the psychics and I had an instant connection. During a break, I walked down the hall to her room to continue the conversation we had started. She was not busy and invited me in.

We talked for a few minutes and I said, "I have to go, I am not feeling well."

"Are you okay?"

I said, "No, not really. I am very dizzy! Enough so I might get sick to my stomach."

She said, "Leave the room, and go into the hall. See if that helps."

I did as she instructed. There was a bit of a breeze in the hallway. It felt amazing. I was perspiring a bit but felt better. I told her, "I feel better!"

She laughed and asked, "Were you feeling okay before you came into my room?"

"Yes, I was, but within a few seconds of being in there I felt awful."

"Now that you look and feel better, are you willing to go back in my room?"

I did not see any reason not to, so I did. She waited in the hall. I moved to a different spot in her room, just to have a comparison. Not even five minutes later, I had to leave again. I was as dizzy as I had been before. I went back out into the hall. I had to put my head between my knees this time, I felt so dizzy.

She explained, "When I do a reading I create a vortex in the room."

Confused I asked, "What the hell is a vortex? And why do you crate one?" Not giving her time to answer, I asked, "A better question, what do you do with it?"

She chuckled and said, "A vortex is a mass of air that spins. It looks like a whirlpool in the drain of a sink, but it's in the air. I use them when I do a reading to hold emotions and feelings. It keeps them away from me so I do not feel clouded during a reading. When the reading is over I clean the room by putting all the emotion that has come out during the reading into it. I am shocked that you could feel it, you are very sensitive."

We stepped back into her room just long enough for her to show me the area of the vortex. Then she grabbed me by the arm and dragged me back into the hall. She laughed again and said, "Your eyes were already starting to spin in your head. You are not to come back in my room. I will come see you at your table!"

Feeling better, I finally let go of the door jam. She asked to see my palms. I turned them over and held them out for her. She grabbed my hands and pointed to an area on my right palm. She said, "Here is where it shows me how very sensitive you are, and that your time is coming soon."

"My time, what do you mean by that?"

"Everything you are working toward, the culmination of it is coming."

I was not exactly sure what she meant by her comment. She had a client show up. I never had an opportunity to ask her.

It has been almost three years since this event. My gift has grown and my first book is an international best seller. I would say she was correct.

This event also happened at the fair in Kentucky. The psychics working this show were incredible busy all day. One was able to make a fast stop by my table.

She said, "The spirit of the guy who walked through your bedroom at home was a guy who died on the road, just down from your house. The guy in the hallway of your house, in khaki pants, was a business guy. But, you already knew that."

She walked away. My husband and I looked at each other. He had questions written all over his face. I explained to him, "Remember the guy that rolled his car in the turn and broke his neck? That is the first guy she talked about."

He said, "I remember that car accident, it was sad."

I wrote about this event in my first book.

I remembered the other man. I was in the bathroom, glanced out into the hall and a guy in a polo shirt and khaki pants floated by. Actually, both of those events are in the first book.

Confirmation of an event is always amazing to get, especially, from someone you have never met. She had not read my book.

I have to say thank you to Patti, Chuck, all the amazingly talented, kind people at the fair. The folks of Kentucky extended true Southern Hospitality to us, it was an honor meeting you.

The fair in Kentucky ended by late afternoon. We packed up quickly and hit the road after heartfelt goodbyes. Less than a block from the venue, I felt two taps on my right shoulder. The placement and angle of the tap meant it could only have come from the back seat. I acknowledged it only with a glance. My husband and I were engrossed in good, constructive conversation about the last two days and I did not want to change the subject. Whoever this was did not want to be ignored and within minutes of the shoulder tap, the taps started on the top of my head. One, two, three taps! This time, I interrupted our conversation and told him what had been happening. He cracked up, then I followed him in laughter. He asked, "What or who do you think it is and why are they tapping you?"

I said, "Maybe it is the building ghost, he could have hitched a ride. I think he simply wants to say good-bye!"

"I guess he liked us. That Southern hospitality is really ingrained!"

We both laughed at that, it's so true.

Still hours from home, my cell phone rang. It was our son, "How long until you are home?"

We laughed, both thinking he was going to be doing a mad dash of house cleaning. He continued before I could even answer, "Because I am trying to concentrate on homework but the house spirits are walking up and down in the hall. Then they step into my room, turn around and leave."

I said, "You need to tell them to knock it off and leave you alone. Say it with meaning. I have homework to do, you all have to leave!"

We hung up. My husband glanced at me and waited for an explanation of that conversation. I relayed the conversation. He simply shook his head in disbelief. It had been a big couple of days for him.

Another thirty minutes went by and my cell phone ring again. "Mom, I did what you told me to do and the house immediately went quiet and has stayed that way. What was their deal?"

"To be honest Son, I am not sure. I am proud of how you handled yourself with the spirits. We will be home soon. Good job!"

Nothing else happened for him and it was quiet for us as, well, after we arrived home. I did not know what to expect. Would it stay quiet or were they mad I had gone away? Sometimes we never get answers.

###

This turns out to me an interestingly quirky day, especially for my husband. It is a great example of how the Universe works in mysterious ways!

My husband, our dog and I, went for a walk in the neighborhood south of our house. We live on a busy road so we have adopted that neighborhood for walks. Right away we ran into one of the residents who lives near the neighborhood entrance. He had purchased my first book. I asked him, "Have you finished it yet?"

He said, "Well…"

Interrupting I said, "I'm afraid to hear what that means!"

My husband and I looked at each other. I know my husband was more afraid of what he was going to too say then I was. My skin was getting thicker by this time, a good thing actually.

Our neighbor looked at us and said, "My first wife was a psychic."

You could have knocked us over with a feather. We have known this man for years, and did not know he had previously been married. It was not a secret, it had simply never come up in conversation. I was not sure if it was public knowledge that the first wife was a psychic, but it might be now!

While we were digesting the new information he said, "Yes I liked your book."

We talked about generalities for a few more minutes. We left and continued our walk.

On the next block we came upon another of the neighbors that we know. She was out walking her dog too. We chatted for a minute or two, and then she begins to tell us about a psychic experience she had had with her ex-husband. I slid a sideways glance at my husband. I knew I would find looking at me. I smiled at him.

Again, someone we have known for several years, and we just found out she was married before, too!

We said good-bye, and moved on around the loop in the subdivision. About a quarter of a mile from home I said to my husband, "There will be one more."

He looked at me and said, "One more what?"

"Items of information or news that is shockingly new to us. They always come in threes. At least in my world they do."

He said, "Oh great. You mean were not home free yet?"

We rounded a corner, and one of the kids in the neighborhood who loves our dog bolted out of the house to say hi! Our dog, Lola returned the love. I asked the girl how school was going. Things sounded great, which made us happy. She had lost her mom five years earlier, it was very tragic.

While we were chatting I noticed the pendent necklace she was wearing. It was beautiful. I had never seen her wear it before. I asked, "What does the symbol on the pendent mean?"

Her hand went to it in a loving way and she said, "The

three small circles on the inside are me and my two brothers. The larger circle that encompassed those small ones represented my father and my new step mom." WHAM! Here was number three. We did not know her dad had remarried. It was happy news.

As we made our way up the street, my husband said, "Let's hurry home before more people come out to talk to us!"

I laughed and said, "Don't worry, there will not be any one else." I was right.
.

###

GROWTH AND ACCEPTANCE

CHAPTER 1

A LIFE WELL AND TRULY LIVED

This event taught me more about life, loss, love, pain and my gifts, than anything else.

My loving, caring, sweet, generous, patriotic, hard laughing, hard working father gently passed away early one morning in June of 2013. I have never felt so numb, more hollowed out, empty.

I was with him when he died, along with my mom, my brothers and eight of my parent's grandchildren. We surrounded his bed as we watched him leave to go home to God and Heaven.

We stood hip to hip, arms around each other, guarding our troubadour. Each of us talked to him, saying good bye for now. We told him it was okay to let go of this world. We assured him he would be safe. We thanked him for loving us so much and always taking the time whenever any of us needed him. As we prayed and talked, he gently passed into God's waiting arms. It was symbolic. It was the way he lived his life, with class and grace. He left us with great thoughts of our time together.

In the last few years, Dad had become more centered. He was at ease with his life and his inevitable death. He and I talked many times over those years about life, living, God, death and Heaven. At one of our get togethers, he told me that he was no long afraid to die. Our conversations had helped him achieve a calm feeling about it and he was at peace. He liked knowing that he was passing to something else. He reached across the table, took my hand and said, "I want to thank you for helping me understand that we do not die alone. That all will be well and joyous on the other side." I smiled from ear to ear. Hearing those words from my dad was truly life affirming. It was a gift.

I told him, "The peace you're feeling is the gift you have given yourself. You simply allowed yourself to receive it."

As I stood by my dad as he was dying, I became incredible dizzy. I looked up to his head and could see a swirling vortex in the air above him. The vortex rose, and it became the shape of a helix (a spiral structure). The helix was a golden color and had champagne-like liquid coursing through its tubular structure. This structure rose up about two feet into the air, then faded into the ceiling of the hospital room.

I was honored to witness my dad's soul leaving his body and ascending to God. My dad was going home! To actually see this happen made me appreciate my amazing and supreme gift.

What I saw that day profoundly touched me. It has changed the way I look at and approach everything, as it should. It was as it was meant to be.

Rest In Peace Dad. I love you and thank you for everything. You lived one hell of a life. I am proud to have been a
part of that life as your daughter. You did good!

I have been hesitant about including this next event. It was
an incredibly private moment known only to my husband
and son. With the intention of open disclosure about growth
and acceptance, I will share what my Spirit Guide had to say.

I went with my parents to most of my dad's many doctors
appointments prior to his heart valve surgery. It was my hon-
or to help them during this trying time. I have always appreciated the love, care and concern they have always shown me.
It was my turn to do that for them.

Much as anyone would, before a major surgery, my dad had
some feelings of trepidation. We had conversations about his
choices, and he came to the conclusion that he really did not
have any other option than to proceed with the surgery. The
doctors, my mom and I agreed with him. He would not have
lived another six months without surgery.

The morning of the surgery starts with a delay due to an
emergency involving my dad's doctor and another patient.
The several hour delay provided my dad some special time
spent with one of his dearest friends. My dad was eventually
taken into the operating room. Five hours later, the surgeon
reported that everything went perfect and we would be able
see him soon. After we visited with him, we headed home to
get some much needed rest.

When we arrived in the Cardiac Intensive Care Unit the
next morning, we found my dad sitting in the chair next to

his bed. He looks up at my mom and me with a huge smile. He said to me, "You knew I would survive!"

I was able to smile at him and say, "Yes I did." I knew he would survive the operation, but I also knew he would not survive the recovery. I was struggling and in denial about what I thought I knew. I was carrying so much guilt, it was making me ill. I shared my guilt with my husband and son. I told them everything, they told me to let it go.

My dad did, in fact, leave us only 24 hours later. There was nothing anyone could have done. Even with this supposed information, I did not know what would take him from us. Trust me, had my spirit guide been specific, I would have shouted the information from the mountain tops to save him. Nobody was at fault for my dad's death, and there wasn't anything we could do to change the outcome. The surgery simply proved to be too much for him at 85 years old.

###

CHAPTER 2

WAITING FOR MY DAD

"We can spend a lifetime waiting. When what we were looking and waiting for, was right before our eyes."
~Exie Susanne Smith

After my dad passed away, I became uninterested in journaling. The thought of doing so was emotionally painful. This was an odd feeling to have about something I had enjoyed doing my entire life.

Paranormal activity had been high for weeks, and each was worthy of a journal entry. None of the activity during that time was documented, so I was not able to include them in this book. They are lost forever. I came to the realization I was waiting for my Dad to appear. I could feel energy building, and hoped it would be the spirit of my dad. Sadly, it was not.

I needed to see his spirit, know that he was okay and be assure he had gone home to Heaven. In my heart, I know the answers already, but I wanted to see him. My dad and I had agreed to visit the other when one of us passed. I guess not.

And then it began to happen. I began to feel his energy. It was subtle at first. I repeatedly felt something like a feather brushing my arm. I said, "Dad, please come and see me. Let me know, by seeing you, that you are okay. I want to know what this is like."

Not getting a reply, I went down the hall, to the laundry room. On the way back to the living room, it felt as if I had passed through several cobwebs. Of course, there were no webs to be seen, but I felt them. I have heard about this phenomenon but never experienced it before. It happened at least 3 more times that day, then stopped as suddenly as it started.

When I told my husband about these events, he looked at me as if I was slow witted. I said, "I am being so silly about this. I am getting so many signs a day, they must be from my dad."

These events were not any like any other I had ever experienced. They were tender, gentle and patent. This was my dad's style, I know it was him. I consulted with my Spirit Guide and she said, "Yes, it is your dad."

I was numb from the loss of my dad. I am sure I missed other signs from him. I probably missed the initial ways he was trying to get my attention, possibly why the feather feeling on my arm. It was so persistent. He really wanted me to receive his message. I am thankful he kept trying.

Thank you Dad. I love you.

While attending a psychic event, I opened one of my books and began to read. The content reminded me of my dad. Under my breath, I said, "I miss you Dad." Exactly at that moment, I felt a soft touch across my left cheek.

The psychic seated at the table next to me turned her head around and asked, "Are you all right?"

I smiled and said, "I am was fine." I loved that she knew something had just happened.

She smiled back at me, "That was special."

It was and knew I did not need to reply.

The interesting interactions with electricity continue. In my first book, I talked about events with light bulbs going out and, on occasion turning back on. This event happened one morning after I had slept really well. I went to sleep talking to my dad and I said good morning to him as soon as I woke up. I kindly told him it would be nice if he came for a visit.

I walked into the kitchen for coffee, and turned on the pendent counter lights. The one closest to me suddenly when out. I thought it odd but it simply could have been its time to die. With skepticism, I said, "If that was something other than the bulb finding its end, do it again for me."

Since I do not believe in coincidence I had to say that. I normally do not issue challenges, it seems rude. Also they always seem to be a predetermined loss for me. For some reason, possibly a lack of coffee, I was compelled to throw down the gauntlet! With the new bulb screwed into place I turned the switch on. Damn! Nothing happened. Not that I thought it would, but honestly I hoped it would! I moved on, poured my coffee, then turned from the refrigerator and back. The same bulb went out just as I looked at it.

I replaced that bulb, again, but decided to first test it in a nearby lamp. It did not light, but it was a new bulb. It could have been a bad bulb, it happens. I tried a third bulb, from a different pack, screwed it into the kitchen light. It worked! I spoke out loud to my spirit guide, "This was odd. Is something going on I should be aware of?" No response was given.

Two days later, I was in the bathroom brushing my teeth. My attention was drawn to my right, and just as I looked at the wall plug, I watched the ground fault button push in and shut the power off. The night light went out and killed the bulb. With a mouth full of tooth paste suds, I said out loud, "Stop playing with my electricity already. I am not made of light bulbs!"

Thankfully nothing has happened like this since.

This event happened one year on Christmas Eve. It was the first time we had not made plans for this particular holiday. Of course, there were not many business or restaurants open that night. We finally found a Chinese return that was open and picked up some carry out to take home. That night, we ate in the living room, on dinner trays watching a Mel Brooks movie. It was nontraditional but fun, nonetheless. After the movie ended, I headed toward my bedroom.

I began talking to my dad while I was changing into my pajamas. I said, "Dad, if you are here with us tomorrow for

Christmas, will you please let us know?" As soon as I finished that request, I turned toward my dresser. The television that sits on the dresser randomly shut itself off. Then, after a three-second delay, the cable box also shut itself off.

There I was, in a pitch dark room, frozen in place. My eyes adjusted to the darkness and then I noticed the lights in the hall were on. I could also hear sounds coming from the living room television. We had not lost power! But, why did everything just shut off in the bedroom?

I turned on my bed side lamp, found the remote controller and turn everything back on. It all worked fine. Perhaps my dad was simply saying, "Merry Christmas" by shutting off the television and cable box. I believe it was him.

Nothing like this has ever happen before or happened since.

I was seated on the couch, deeply focused on writing this book, when I noticed something out of the corner of my eye. I saw a full body apparition drift across the hallway, from left to right.

It occurred to me, this new spirit was a different shade of black than the others I have seen in the house. We have a residential, male spirit that appears to me as a solid black mass. The new spirit is not as dark and dense, but it is also the shape of a man. This new apparition is taller, thinner and not as dense. We have another haunt, this one residual that appears back in that area of the house. However, he always appears in full color.

After I witnessed this movement, I also heard a noise, a click. One of the ceramic tiles in the back hall had come loose. It makes a clicking noise when you walk on it. I heard that tile click; someone had just walked on it.

I looked down the hall, no one was there. Or so I thought. Then I saw a blur of movement, the blur that turned into a black outline. The spirit simply stood there looking back at me, then it was gone. I clearly recognized the outline and height, it was my dad. I would know it anywhere.

The next day, I was again working on my book while seated on the couch. Another blurred movement but this one moved across the kitchen. I asked, "Who are you? How about coming out here in the living room with me?" I waited a few minutes for something to happen, like movement or a noise. I said, "Is this you dad, are you back?" Nothing happened, nothing moved, no noise.

In my head I heard my Spirit Guide tell me. "It was your dad. He wants to make sure you put him in this book!" I started to laugh. I then heard her say, "You would never and will never forget him." This started the tears flowing. I asked my Spirit Guide to please make sure he knows how much he means to me and that, of course, he will be in my book. She did.

Dreams, in my opinion, are entirely personal and subjective. I am including dreams as "events" because they are keys, windows to our lives, messages for us and food for the soul. We tend to remember the important ones.

In this dream, my husband and I were thrust into a country

setting. We were on vacation, driving our car on a country road, when a van pulled up alongside us. They were signaling for us to pull over and stop. Unlike what we would have done in real life, we actually pulled the car over to the side of the road and stopped. We jumped out of the car and ran to the right side door of the van.

I knew my dad was inside the van. I heard a voice in my head say, "Your dad is so glad to be getting out for a ride."

The side door of the van slid open. It was a 1970s style stretch van. Back then, the only back seat door, was a side door on the right. I knew exactly where to get in and hopped up onto the bench seat in the second row. No one was in the driver's seat. There was someone in the front passenger's seat. The person in that seat turned and looked directly at me. He had a huge smile on his face, it was my dad! He looked fit, happy and in his mid 30's. I had been asking and waiting for him to appear for me in a dream.

I love you, Dad, and miss your presence in our lives more than words can say.

###

CHAPTER 3

SPIRITS AND SPIRIT GUIDES

I am fortunate to have found a workout class that I share with a fantastic group of women. As I say, I like to suffer en masse! Our glorious leader is a gifted, strong woman that fires us up and makes us laugh. We work out in the gymnasium of a religious school which is physically attached to the church. Both the church and school are always bustling with activity.

During one of our workout sessions, I notice people coming in and out of the old kitchen in the back of the gym. They were carrying coffee and water, obviously setting up for an event. I overheard another woman in my workout class say, there was a funeral service scheduled in the sanctuary that morning. Upon hearing this, I had thoughts of wonder about possible spirits inhabiting the church and school. However, I have never seen a spirit in the countless times I have been there. That was about to change.

We all have our favorite "spots" in the gym we use for the classes. My "spot" is approximately ten feet away from the room we store our weights and floor mats in. Most of the time, the doors are kept closed. But on this day they were both wide open and the ceiling light was on. I was lying on my mat, doing abdominal crunches, when I noticed shadow movement in the storage room.

It captured my attention so I stared into the room for a while. Maybe somebody was in the room? Well, no one that was alive. Again, I saw shadow movement, a large dark shadow that moved in front of wood shelves. I am thankful the music was turned up so loud, because I made an "Oh!" sound and slight gasp for air. No one heard me, so no questions.

I did not see any further shadow movement but kept an eye on that storage room for the rest of the workout. It was a bit distracting, I am far too curious to ignore out of place shadows.

I guess who ever it was just wanted to see what we were doing, and popped in.

I work diligently, every morning, at tuning into my Spirit Guide. I took the advice of a psychic I met several months ago, she said, "Shut up and listen!" She meant I needed to quiet my mind. I have a hard time in that area, my mind seems to work all the time.

She suggested, "When you first wake up, ask your spirit guide what you need to know for the day. Listen, pay attention to the first thoughts that come into your mind. Those thoughts are from your spirit guide." Since I have incorporated her advice in my daily life, it has become easier to focus on the assistance from my spirit guide. Once I began to trust my spirit guide, I started to ask her specific questions.

One morning while checking in for the day, I asked if I would have time to write that day. What I heard back was, "You will have all the time you want tomorrow. Do not squander it."

As my day continued, everything I did worked out, surprisingly, exactly as it should. It seemed possible that the following day would be entirely free for me to write all day. But then I discovered we needed something for the next day and that would require a trip to the grocery store. An interruption! I looked to the heavens for help.

Just then my husband yelled from the kitchen, "Good news, I found a pound of coffee in the freezer! I swear it was not there yesterday."

I do not believe spirits have the ability to put food in the freezer, so, of course, it was already there. However, I certainly appreciate the fact that I would still be on track to write the next day. My spirit guide had told me to trust her but my nature is to worry about even small distractions.

The next morning, I awoke to a special song playing on the radio. The song's lyrics were what encouragement me when I began writing my first book. It had been playing repeatedly until I sat down to write that book. Here it was again, encouraging me to spend my day writing. It was a beautiful start to a productive day.

I converse with my Spirit Guide daily. I now find it like talking with counsel, a great, close friend. There is still a learning curve. I have found that words can be put into your head as if it were coming from you guide. I try to remember what I was told, "Trust what you hear or see first. Things that come into your mind after that are usually things that you want to hear or have happen. Not things that necessarily will happen."

One of the messages I heard, but did not want to believe, is that my mom would not live beyond November of 2014. I kept this to myself for several months, before I even told my husband. He did not question it because the information I received about my dad's death was so eerily correct. I hoped I was wrong about this.

On a day in August of 2014, I woke up and asked my spirit guide about the day and about my mom. I heard that the day would be amazing and that my mom would live if things changed. That was all I received. It was a relief to get the message about my mom. My mind began thinking about what I had to do that day. My intentions were to do whatever we need to accomplish the changes necessary to help my mom.

Weeks went by and events were forming that did not bode well for my mom. Her situation did not change, at least not the way I thought it needed to. I tried to stay positive regarding the tests her doctor order. It was amazing how things fell into place! One test result after the other came back, all good. This was an "aha!" moment for me.

I am communicating with my Spirit Guide unquestionably. I am also learning to rely on God. He is here to help, as well.

Thank you, thank you, thank you.

###

CHAPTER 4

LEND A HELPING HAND

Many people contact me looking for answers in their own life. I enjoy offering my knowledge in hopes they find answers to their many questions. This is the primary reason I wrote this book and the last one. I love helping others who are apprehensive, scared or confused about their own gifts.

One such person who contacted me for help was a friend who could no longer attend large functions, it was simply overwhelming to her. Her situation was made even more difficult because her husband did not understand what she was experiencing. She contacted me via social media and asked how to deal with being a sensitive. A "sensitive" is someone who is keenly aware of other people's moods and physical states of being. She described how she is picking up on everyone's feelings in a room. She said her husband was starting to think this was all in her head.

I could completely relate to her circumstances. I offered her advice based on how I learned to survive in large groups of people. I told her, "I imagine in my mind that I am being draped by a king sized sheet of gauze or screening, from head to toe. The idea is to filter out as much crap from other people as possible."

I also told her about using white light. "Imagine standing

under a big light bulb that covers you in white light. This is the light of goodness and protection." I encouraged her to practice protecting herself before going to the grocery store. We ended our conversation, and I prayed for her success.

Several weeks later I asked her, "How are things going? Does one method work better than the other?"

She replied, "I have been practicing both actually, just to be safe. There was a big function that I told my husband I would attend. He was very excited! We went and both had a great time. Thank you so much."

This made my day! I helped this woman rejoin her marriage, and get back out into society.

A long time friend contacted me, again via social media, who also needed my help. She is one of the nicest people I know. She would do anything for anyone, and often does. She made it clear she did not want to be a bother, also true to form. I assured her it was no bother at all, and asked how I could be of assistance.

Her husband had suddenly and tragically passed away only three months earlier. Since then she had been searching for his lost wedding band. She asked me if my psychic gifts could help find her husband's ring. I was stunned by the request and the level she was asking me to reach. I told her that I would try, and contact her if I had something to report.

I turned off the television, made the house completely quiet, and sat in a comfortable spot on the couch. I leaned back into the cushions, closed my eyes, and spoke out loud to her husband's spirit and my spirit guide, "Please show me where your wedding band is, so I can tell your wife, and she can be at peace with this. Thank you to whoever is helping me."

In my mind, I was now in a kitchen with white cabinets and vintage black hinges. The counter came out toward me from the wall. Beyond that, to the left of the counter was a dark room. I knew, without seeing it, that it was the mud and laundry room. Her husband's landscaping truck was parked just outside. This was where he went to and from work. I gazed down at the counter, and behind a white toaster, there was a shinning blurry circle. Instantly, I knew it was his ring, I found it!

I contacted my friend to tell her what I saw. She said, "Yes, you are right about everything except the color of the toaster. Right before he died, we got a stainless steel one to replace the broke white one..."

She abruptly interrupted her own sentence and said, "I know where it is!" She promptly hung up the phone.

I understood she was filled with excitement when she realized and remembered the location of the ring. She left me hoping, she would find his ring. A few hours later, not being able to wait any longer, I called her. I realized this conversation could have a flip side to it, joy or disappointment.

With my heart in my throat, she answered the phone. I said, "Well?"

"Yes, I found it, but not on the counter."

The only response I could muster was, "Oh."

She said, "I did not mean to disappoint you. It had been in that exact spot on the counter for years. Roughly a month before he died, we decided he did not need to keep taking it off for work and putting it back on when he got home. The decision was for him to wear it for special occasions, so we put it back in the original ring box and placed that in the bottom layer of my jewelry box. That is where I found it."

We talked a bit longer and while we did, she confined everything I told her. In all the years I have known her; I have never been in her home. For her to tell me I got the kitchen and mud room exactly right was amazing.

Just before we hung up she said, "I would never have found it if you had not said it was on the counter. I knew the minute you said that exactly where I needed to look. Thank you."

My heart was pounding through my chest when I put the phone down. I felt like I had just run a race and won! The adrenalin rush from this was new to me and incredible.

I sat back down on the couch and said out loud, "Thank you for the help in locating the ring. Thank you for helping me help a friend, in distress."

I sat in the quiet for a long while, thinking how I made this happen. For years I have been wanting this ability to bloom, it finally did. Everything happens when it is supposed to.

Having worked on the computer all afternoon, I took a break and visited my social network page. I looked at different pages and posts, and then a picture that literally jumped off the screen at me. I was taken aback at how much this picture spoke to me. I could tell just by looking at it, the house in the photo, was haunted. I was so preoccupied with the picture; I had not yet read the caption attached to the photo. It read, "Looking for help. What do you see in the photo?"

I looked closely at it again I could not see any spirits with my eyes, but I felt that something was there. At first I felt one spirit, a child, I thought. Then I thought no, but realized I was picking up a second spirit. It was an adult, possibly a Native American.

I posted a note to her about the two spirits I felt were in here home. There were other posts before and after mine. Some were trying to sooth and comfort her, some talked of demons, and one attacked my post. I thought whatever, I know what I am picking up and hope she is okay. Just as I was leaving the page, I got a private message, from the woman that posted the picture.

She said, "Thank you for the calm head about this, can we chat?"

I replied, "Yes we can chat. Please know that I am not trying to sell you anything. I simply would like to help, if I can. Contact me at your convenience."

She replied immediately, "I do not have spirits in my home. I have been very ill for over a month. I was hoping someone could tell me what is wrong with me."

I said, "I am sorry, I cannot do that."

Her last note, "I am sorry to have bothered you."

I realized this woman was distress and need help, but what could I do? I went to her page on social media, looking for clues about her situation. I needed to see if I could glean anything. Was she mentally ill? Abused? Depressed? To the contrary, her page was happy, light and full of love. This helped me decide, it was spirit, not in her head.

I typed her a note asking, "How long have you lived in this house? I must tell you, I do believe you have spirit activity in your home." I had the nerve to add I thought she should get a complete physical. Yikes, I have some nerve!

To my surprise she answered my note. She said, "We have been here for six month. I have not heard or seen anything unusual in the house. I will be honest, it feels weird, though."

I thought okay, now we are getting some place. She has a bit of a gift and is ignoring it. Sounds familiar.

She inquired, "Are you picking up anything else?"

"I am and I think you need to have a shaman come in to do a blessing and sage the house. You know something is up, you know this in your gut. You need to pay attention to this feeling and trust it because you are correct. One spirit is young, a child, and the other is an older, Native American male. Also, I think he is a haunting of the land. Is your house built on or near sacred land."

She asked, "If I pray hard enough will my Spirit Guide come and help me? If I have one that is."

"Oh you have one, we all do. She is communicating with you, so slow down and listen, you will hear her." I was shaking my head at myself, this statement from me was prophetic.

I told her, "You really need to get the house blessed." Then I asked, "Do you live near a grave yard or church?"

That was the last note exchanged for several hours, but then she replied, it blew me away! She said, "I contacted the church next door and explained what was going on in my home. The woman who answered the phone said they would have to call me back."

She then said, "Oh sorry, I just saw your note. Yes, I live next door to a church."

My mouth dropped open, I knew that. I waited by my computer for a note back from her, hoping the church group would not let her down. A note finally showed up, "The person I talked to at the church just called back, she and others are coming over now!"

Taking a big deep breath, I typed back, "I am so glad. Please let me know how it goes."

Her last note to me, after the people from the church were gone, said, "They prayed in the house, some were even speaking in tongues. It has seemingly helped, the house feels lighter and looks brighter. Thank you for taking the time for me."

Later that same evening, I received a note from her. She was still considering having the house blessed and doing a sage burning by Native American Shaman. She hoped that would cover everything. I thought it a good idea and said that in a note I sent back.

This type of event has been recently happening more often. It feels good to help.

To this day, she still communicates with me via social networking. Once in a while, she posts a smiley face to my page. It makes my day and lets me know she is okay.

I randomly received a call from an employee of my first publishing company. She reached out for help, and guidance, but disguised it as a business call. She worked in the marketing department, noticed my book, and called with some advertising idea. What I assumed was going to be another bothersome call, turned into something quite different.

When I answered that call, she asked for me, and then introduced herself. She said, "Is there anything you need from us or that we can do for you Exie?" I thought it odd, yet kind. Then the other shoe fell. She said, "I saw your book in our catalog and did an abbreviated read. I love it, will read the rest, but have questions for you, if you don't mind?"

"Well," seemed to be all I could say at first. "Thank you, I am glad it grabbed your attention from the catalog."

The second I took a breath to say more, she jumped in and started rifling questions at me. This lasted for an hour! At the time, I did not realize our conversation had lasted so long.

It is a topic of choice for me, so I let her go on. She is gifted, psychically, and like so many others, she wanted my confirmation. I understand the insecurity associated with paranormal gifts, so I am happy to tell them what they need to hear.

Our conversation was going along fine, until she asking my advice about a specific situation. Before I could stop her and decline offering my advice, she began telling me the details. I attempted to speak, but she kept talking. I could have hung up the phone, but she had gone so far out her way to reach me. I decided to listen.

She began by saying, "Should I leave my apartment because there is a spirit in it?"

I asked, "What spirit?" I thought whoa, she had not mentioned a spirit up until now. This is weird and was going to get weirder. "Why would you leave? Is the spirit bothering you? I think you already know what you need to do. Why are you asking me?"

She talked right over me and added, "My grandfather thinks I need to move."

Curious, I asked, "Why does he say you should move?"

She talked fast, and told me about how sick she had been. "I have been hospitalized three times in a short amount of time. He thinks it is a spirit making me ill, so I should leave the apartment." Her story is a classic escalation of paranormal energies that usually culminate with the person getting sicker as time goes on.

Once she explained, I decided she was not mentally ill. It

was her apartment or actually what was in her apartment, that was making her ill. Since it could have been something other than spirit, I asked about mold and other potential culprits. She assured me that all the test were done and everything check out okay.

I looked at the clock. I was shocked when I realized how long we had been on the phone. I interrupted her, "I really do have to go. It sounds like your grandfather is right, you need to move, get out."

Before we hung up, I requested she let me know how she was doing once she moved. It has been months, and I have not heard from her. I hope and pray she is alive and well.

I received an email from a woman, "A friend of my mother's has a spirit in her house and wants to know what she should do."

I replied, "What does she want to do with it? Does she simply want to set rules for it but let it stay? Does she want it to go away? All of these are possibilities. Please ask her, and let me know. I will give her direction then based on her response."

I never heard back from her. I am left to assume her friend's mother has chosen to live with the spirit.

A childhood friend of mine sadly lost her mother. I learned of this from a social network post. I left my friend a note of sympathy. She lived on the other side of the country, so she was unable to visit with her mother before she passed away. My friend was distraught. I deeply felt her pain because I had just lost my father six months prior. Along with my sympathy, I offered suggestions of ways to contact her mom for some closure.

My cell phone rang; I did not recognize the area code. I answered anyway.

"Hi, I cannot believe you posted that note about my mom. She came to see me in a dream last night. My mom and I talked, it was wonderful. She had not been able to speak for quite a while, you see."

In my post, I had suggested that she ask her mom to come see her in a dream. Not having talked with this woman for many years, I was relieved that she is open to that line of spiritual thinking. She then told me a bit of what they talked about, past and current topics in her life.

I asked her, "How did you feel when you woke up?"

She said, "I felt calm, lighter, and more at peace then I have in a while. Why do you ask?"

I told her, "I think that your dream was real, that you were really conversing with your mom. I have been lucky enough to have this happen a few times to me in my life. When I awake from one of these sessions, I feel energized and have a level of happiness that matches no other." I also said, "There is no proof of this. It is a feeling, like so many others, I trust and believe in. So, I must this one as well. What do you think?"

"It was real," is all she said.

We hung up, I thought of her often over the next few days. No one warns you how tough it is or how much it hurts to lose a parent. Possibly because no one can express this level of hurt.

"All things come to he who waits."
                                ~Violet Fane (1843-1905)

The quote is correct, but it is usually misquoted, "All good things come to those who wait." Either way, the sentiment is the same. Truthfully, nothing comes without working for it. We must have patience.

This is not easy for me. I dislike waiting, but have learned lessons on patience from certain situations that have been put in front of me. I believe challenges will continue until I learn better ways of coping with impatience. This is part of my life long education, things my soul needs to learn this time back. How we achieve life education is through reincarnation, we return as many times as it takes to learn and educate the soul. Everyone has a reason, or reasons, they come back. Do you know what your soul has come back to learn?

As a child, I use to wonder what I was doing here. Did I have a reason, other than being miserable? I was not an overly happy child. As I got older, I learned about frustration and what triggered it for me. About ten years ago, I came to realize I had come back, to learn patience, with myself and with others. Trust me, I am a work in progress. Some days I can only take baby steps toward that goal, but I continue the quest.

The following event has multiple parts, each important. It is amazing what one conversation can do for your life. I had patiently waited for this without even realizing it!

The wonderful couple who currently live in my childhood home, love it as much as our family did. When I spoke with the wife, she mentioned both her and her husband immediately knew something was different about the house.
They purchased it anyway.

The female homeowner was very hesitant about sharing the following information with me. I thank God she did.

She said, "A friend of mine unexpectedly came into town earlier in the week. She usually stays in the guest room. Since we did not know she was coming, I had already put granddaughter in that room. My friend would have to use the basement accommodations. She was okay with that."

Her guest woke the next morning, ate and was on her way. The following day, the houseguest called her to inform her about a spirit that had bothered her while she was staying in the basement.

When she told me this, my mouth must have been hanging open in shock! I was barely able to contain my emotions as I asked, "Did she say anything else?"

"Not until I asked her how the spirits presence felt, good or bad?"

Her friend said, "I got a chilling, scary feeling. I think he did not like me down there in the basement."

"Your friend said, he?"

"Yes, said it was a boy."

She then asked, "What do I do now Susanne? Advice would be greatly appreciated."

I went on to tell the home owner, "Your friend's description of this spirit is very familiar, he is a bully, but not evil. Besides, you have lived in the house long enough to know if he were evil."

We talked about smudging the entire house. She called me later that same day, "We have decided to smudge the house, I have the sage."

"That is a great idea, it cannot hurt. Remember to get in the corners and behind furniture. Good luck!"

We talked again a few days later. She said the house felt oaky, but the dog was not happy in one part of the living room. He growls at thin air. She assumes something is there that she could not see. I asked her if it was a certain area and she said yes. I had always felt a presence in that exact place when we lived in the house.

This spirit is basically a basement dweller. He would play on the stairs, occasionally come into the kitchen and the edge of the dining room. He hangs back two or three feet into the shadow of that room. He is why I always felt watched, and that is what is bothering her dog.

I emailed her the next day to check on her. She said she thought the smudge had been successful, so far anyway. This news made me feel better for them.

I used the word "smudge" in this event. I will be including the definition of that word in the glossary, but wanted to talk more about it here. To "smudge" or do a "smudging" is a Native American tradition to cleanse. The most widely used technique is with a tied bundle of sage. You light the bundle with a lighter or match, at one end. When the flame is tamped out, you only get smoke from the hot embers. The smoke is the purifier. You bless yourself first, then take the smoking sage into every room of the dwelling. Be sure to reach up high, go low under any furniture, and in corners and closets. The smoke attaches to the spirit and as the smoke dissipates, it takes the spirit with it.

In this case, they utilized it as a spirit-cleansing tool. Smudging can also be used to bless a location, person or an object. It can also remove negativity. When doing a smudging, your intention should be clear, and you should remain positive and peaceful.

The phone call about this event was incredibly important in my life. It confirms my past and lends credence to all my experiences.

###

CHAPTER 5

SPIRIT VISITS NOT AT HOME

We have a group of friends that we do all sorts of fun activities with. On this particular weekend, we planned a "girls only" get-away. One of the couples has a charming cottage in the middle of Michigan, so we decided to go there. Our plans were simple: relaxation, wine, conversation and food, with evening bonfires. And not necessarily in that order!

One night, the conversation ebbed and flowed in the usual non-stop fashion, covering many topics. Inadvertently, we began discussing death and loss. One of the women in the group had recently lost a sibling. They had a close relationship, so she was understandably struggling. Everyone in the group has siblings, so we tried to put ourselves in her shoes. We offered as much compassion as possible.

I had a feeling she wanted to say something to me. Later, we spoke privately. I told her how sorry I was about my family missing her brother's memorial service due to the fact we in Europe at the time. We learned about his death after we returned from our trip. I did not think we were so special she would remember we were going away, and indeed she had forgotten. She said she wondered why we had not attended the viewing or service, but now understood. My gut was correct. She had been a bit "standoffish" because she was hurt. I was glad we cleared that up.

As the evening continued, she told us more about her bother and we learned his death was sudden, a shock to the entire family. I think it is more difficult to cope with a death when you do not have a chance to say good bye. They were robbed of that opportunity.

Just as the topic of conversation changed, a huge black moth came fluttering madly into view. Not surprisingly, it landed on the shoulder of the woman who was grieving so heavily. I knew how much she hated bugs, so I shot out of my chair to shoo it away. But there was nothing there, not on her, her chair or the ground around her. I sat back down feeling confused. I know what I saw, and it was different from any moth I had never seen. My radar clicked on, something was up or going to be. This had meaning.

The fire was dying out and we were worn out, time for bed. We gathered up our things and headed in doors. I was the first to reach the sliding glass door. When I went to open it, my gaze went inside. My attention was drawn straight ahead to the end of a short hall. Something moved across it in shadow form. I was standing still, the others had yet to make it over to the door. The movement I saw was not from us. Who was it? I had been at this cottage several times and never had experienced feelings of spiritual activity there.

I opened the sliding door, from left to right. I saw the shadow at the end of the hall move again. Interesting, the shadow moved after the door opened, right to left. I paused for a moment in the door way, waiting to see if the shadow was going to come out and play or simply tease. Nothing else happened, which was okay, I had no desire to bring my friends into a situation that would have frightened them, at least not without warning them first. This made me smile, I love the validation I feel when I see a spirit some place other than at home.

We straightened up the main level of the house and headed for bed. Three of us were up in the one bedroom loft. I was given the small bedroom and two others were just feet away in bunk beds, one of them was our grieving friend. Without any further thought about the shadow from down stairs, I washed my face, changed and fell into bed.

I woke up, and the house was pitch black. I reached for my phone to check the time. It was 2:38 a.m., the house was utterly quiet, too quiet, actually. A song started to play in my mind. This was not just any song. It was the song that played for both of my girlfriends, one after her death and the other as she lay dying. I put my phone back on the nightstand, I laid my head back onto the pillows and looked into the darkness toward the foot of the bed. About one and half feet from the end of the bed was a chest of drawers. A spirit, in the shape of a person was not standing in from of that chest. I knew, by instinct this was the spirit that had caused the shadow movement down stairs. It is the spirit of my friend's sibling.

In my head, I heard, "Please tell her I love her, have always loved her. Tell her I said thank you for everything she has always done for me and to watch for me, because I will come to see her."

In my thoughts, I promised him I would tell her. I laid there for a while, after the shadow had gone away. I wondered, how does one tell a "still seriously hurting" sibling something like this?

I was the first one awake the next morning. I needed coffee and time to think, I headed down stairs. Still contemplating my strategy to approach the situation, I heard the others wake up. I did not want to make her cry, but knew this would. I also wanted to make sure she knew I was sincere.

I assumed she believes in my gifts and that I only want what is best for her. I waited for her to get a cup of coffee, I got my third. Since I had been given a message that I promised to deliver, I dove right in. When everyone was awake and settled with a morning beverage, I decided this was as good a time as any to start. I said, "Hell, since I really do not know how to start this conversation, I am just going to say it." I had their attention and knew what I was going to say would be unexpected.

I looked directly at my friend and said, "Your sibling was here in the middle of the night and gave me a message for you."

She started to cry, Shit! I managed to keep talking, she needed to hear exactly what he said and quickly. After I was done, she talked for a while about him, about his life. The appreciation on her face was wonderful when I told her he was thankful for everything she had ever done for him. That took away all the fears I had about furthering her pain.

Love and loss brings out deep emotion. My friend received answers that none of us knew she was even seeking. This spiritual communication healed more than pain, between this brother and sister, than I will ever know. I was honored to have been entrusted with this message between siblings, and happy it was accepted well. Thank you both.

###

My husband surprised me, and our son, with a trip to Italy. It was a dual celebration of our 25th wedding anniversary, and our son's graduation from University. We flew into Rome, spent four glorious days touring and eating. I felt pressure from spirit all over the city but nothing showed itself. I thought maybe there was so much energy and spirit activity that I could not differentiate between them. I had basically the same experience during our time in Florence, a lot of energy but nothing materialized. I did feel more spirit activity in Florence.

We traveled from Florence to Venice by train, took a water taxi to St. Marks Square, and walked from there to our hotel, which was just off the square. We had a map, and thought we could easily find the hotel, or so we thought. While standing in St. Mark's Square, in the midst of a crowd of several hundred tourists, we realized the map was incorrect. We could not find the hotel entrance. Imagine us pulling little wheeled suitcase over stone streets (more like paths) with backpacks that are quickly becoming an irritant. We were starting to get a bit short tempered with the situation and each other. We decided to ask a few shop owners if they knew where the hotel entrance was. They had no idea, or simply did not care to help us. We asked more shop owners and were sent in several different directions, to no avail.

I prayed for help. "Please God send us help, we are not able to find the hotel. Silly I know. This trip has been perfect thus far and I do not want to ruin it with short tempers. I wish only joy for our last few days. Thank you." While I was praying, we continued walking and ended up back at the place the computer map pinpointed as the hotel entrance. All I could think was, how can we be so off?

From behind us we heard a voice ask, "Are you lost? You look lost! Is there any way I can help you?" We turned in unison to find an older gentleman with a snow white full beard, a sweet face with pink cheeks, speaking United Kingdom English. He was wearing slacks with large pockets on the legs, a long sleeve shirt, an olive green fishing vest and topping all off a Tyrollean hat, and of course, a feather.

My husband, son and I exchanged looks with one another and smiled. We could not help it. He was quintessential cute. It was Santa Claus, who we suspected, had cut his fishing trip short to help us find our hotel. I knew we were all thinking it.

Without a word, he led us down a walk way to a locked door. We had already tried that door once, but to no avail, since nobody there spoke English. Our kind gentleman knocked, the same woman answered the door as before. He told her our plight. She told us to come in with a wave of her hand. The gentleman bowed his head to her, and then to us as he backed away. We all spoke at the same time, offering heartfelt thanks to the kind gentleman. He smiled at us, wished us a wonderful stay and backed out of sight as the door was closing.

This was not the main entrance, as it turns out. The front desk was contacted, and someone was assigned to help us, the lost tourists, find the main desk. We got even more lost as we made our way through the hotel. After taking stairs up and down twice, then several halls, we ended up at the gorgeous front desk.

Ironically, after we checked in the door we would use on a daily basis was next to the spot we kept ended up while trying to find the main entrance. Once we got into our room, and were alone, I asked, "Did either of you think our gentleman savior looked out of place and a bit like Santa Clause?"

Again we all started to talk at once about him and the situation. It was great!

We were assigned to the Venice Room, which was actually an apartment. We dropped our suitcases and excitedly went out to tour the island known as Venice. I acknowledged the butterflies in my stomach. I assumed they were simply there because I was finally in the city I have wanted to visit my whole life. Touring around, I had a glass of vino, in hopes of calming down. The wine was fantastic but did nothing to rid my gut of the odd feelings I was experiencing. I tried my best to let it go and get lost in the excitement of the city.

I told my family about what I was feeling, they laughed, not at me but about the facts in front of me. They reminded me how old the city is, so spirit energy must be off the charts. We are also surrounded by water, which is a great conductor and enhancer of energy. I was happy with them for the reminder, and for understanding. I hugged and thanked them both.

They were proven correct as we toured the Doges Palace and crossed over the Bridge of Sighs. There was pressure, and an accompanying creepiness, here that had me overwhelmed and dizzy, I had to hang on to my husband's arm a few times. Despite the intense energy and overwhelming sadness on the bridge, I never did see any spirits.

After a glorious day of touring, fabulous food and wine, we dropped on the couch back in the apartment. Our son decided to go back out to see the cities nightlife. My husband was happy to watch a bit of television in the living room. I decided to get ready for bed, relax, and journal about the day. I needed to absorb what seemed more like a dream than reality.

I could hear the television from the living room. My husband was watching an American sit-com in Italian. I thought it funny considering he does not speak Italian. Done journaling about the day, I shut the bed room door, creating a quiet environment for sleep.

It had not been long after I shut my eyes, when the room filled with energy. Suddenly wide awake, as the energy in the room moved back and forth at the foot of the bed. Someone was pacing. The energy felt agitated, upset, and mad. I looked in that direction and the spirit appeared for me. He was quite obviously a spirit. I could see the curtained bank of windows behind him. His mode of dress was ancient, that of the rich and noble. The sprit was male, big and strong, prominent facial features. His nose was very large and hooked down. Even before I could see him, I felt his power and ire. Once he appeared, it confirmed everything I had felt about him. He was tall for his era, had a modern day wrestlers build. He must have been an imposing person in his day. I think, too, with the attitude he was emanating, he was an important person. Maybe he held an office or was possibly a member of the ruling family. His clothing included long flowing robes made from expensive textiles. The colors, I imagine, were only for the royals. I shall never forget the navy blue velvet top robe he was wearing. The color was exquisite.

The way his energy filled the room caused me to expect

another spirit to appear. No others did show up. He was a massive, impressive energy. I studied him as he dramatically paced back and forth about a foot from me. I could see the concentration, anger and ego on his face. I know he did not see me. I imagine the room looked to him the way it did in his time.

As I look back on this experience, I remember how shocked I was to see him. We had been in Italy for nine days and I had not seen a spirit. Fortunately, I was able to see him in my own private theater. I will never forget his grand gestures. Before he could turn, he had to grab a handful of the back of his glorious robe and fling it behind him. He was quite a sight.

Eventually, I rolled over on my side, pulling the covers over my head, and went to sleep. The spirit was gone when I woke up in the morning. I wondered if he was still pacing but maybe I could not see him in the day's light. I knew the answer actually. He was gone, along with the incredible energy.

During breakfast, my husband asked me why the bed covers were over my head. He knows I do not like to re-breath air, so he was curious. With that conversational opening, I told he and my son about what I had seen the night before. They were as pleased as I was that something had finally shown up.

Day two in Venice proved to be another full and fantastic day. My husband and I parted ways with our son at the end of the day. He wanted to find a night cap and we to collapse in our room. I left my husband in the living room I went to get ready for bed. I wondered if I would see my well-dressed pacing spirit again.

With the bedroom television on, I climbed into bed, hoping to clear my mind for a few minutes. That was not to be. My attention was immediately drawn from the television to the foot of bed. I could feel energy building again. This time, I wanted more information about the spirit. Who he was? I sensed he was middle aged for our time, that would make him old during his time. He was indeed important. This hotel was formerly his home. Since it was only one hundred yards from the palace, I wondered if he was involved in the government. He was worried about something that might not turn out well for him if things continued on their current path. He did not know he was dead. He was in his time, he could not see me. He had a temper and was planning to use it the next couple of days. I got the feeling he loved this life and the life or death games he played.

I am not sure how long I watched him. I would love to know more about who this spirit was. Perhaps someday I will research him, but for now, he remains a magical mystery.

###

As an artist, I love when local people show support. I know a woman who is part owner of a store located in and old farm house. She only sells products made by local artists and authors.

I liked this woman the minute I met her. Frankly, I was a bit jealous of her energy.

While dropping off copies of my book, I was able to meet many of her customers. They were having a great time shopping. After they had all left for the day, the storeowner and I were able to chat for a while.

I was feeling odd since I arrived. Old houses are often crooked and out of plumb, it gives me the fun house effect, a dizzy feeling. This place had a many small rooms, packed to the gills which did not help either. Those theories went out the window when she proceeds to tell me about the ghost in the house! She told me this had been the home of the ghost.

She asked, "Where do you feel her presence?"

I told her, "By the stairs to the second floor. However I do feel her all over on this first floor. Does she go between rooms upstairs? I get the feeling she flies from room to room"

"Yes, she does. Well, at least that is what I feel she does."

While we talked about the stores policies, and how she liked to do business, I heard someone walk around behind me, in the other room. I tried to ignore it, thinking maybe it was a customer who was still in the store. I finally looked into that room, but did not see anyone. I could see out into the parking lot, the only car parked outside was mine. As I looked into the room again, I heard more footsteps. The room was empty and the upstairs was closed off to the public.

I asked the owner, "Do people hear someone walking around in the entry room?"

She said, "Oh yes, quiet often."

"Count me as one of them! I just heard her walking around in there."

This was a great time to leave. We smiled shook hands, and said good-bye. The store is a cool place, and she is a kind hearted woman for helping local people sell their creations.

###

CHAPTER 6

SPIRITS AT HOME

When I tell someone I have had a weird day, I am not sure they can even imagine what that really means. This was a weird day, even for me, and that makes me chuckle. My life is wonderfully interesting, and this spirit visitation is a perfect example.

Our household's residual haunt has been extremely busy. He has been moving back and forth in the hall more than usual. Besides his energy in the house, I felt and saw, a semi-solid human shaped spirit in my kitchen. He has been popping in and out. The first time I noticed him was while I was dusting in the living room. I felt a change in energy, looked up, and there he was. Just as quickly, he disappeared.

What was so strange that day was how different the energy felt to me. It rose and fell with a plop, like a water drop falling onto concrete. I stood there for several minutes, staring at thin air. I thought there would be more activity, and that something else would happen. Like I said, odd.

Since my residual haunt, on this day, was not simply energy repeating the set pattern over and over, exactly the same every time, does this make him something other than a residual haunt? Is he now a residential haunt? I think so and I think I owe someone an apology...Wes!

###

I have stated previously, my bedroom is the "Spirit Forbidden Zone." Mostly, I do this for my husband. I do not want him to be bothered while he is trying to sleep. I drape the room in white light, say blessings and pray that only God, angels and our spirit guides enter.

I instituted this because the dead were popping in all the time, any hour day or night. We simply could not live like that. I have not wanted to admit it, but for at least a week, there has been a spirit lurking in the corner of the bedroom. I was lazy, and did not want to deal with it right away. I was hoping it would get bored and move on.

It takes a lot to creep me out, especially in my own home. I had been asleep, but woke up and was not sure why. I laid in bed, on my back, not moving, only listening to the house and the night. Each spirit has noises that are specific only to them. This night there was no noise at all. I could not believe my ears, so I waited a few more heart beats for normal noises to start. Nothing happened. I was about to throw the covers back and get out of bed, when something inside me said to wait.

My senses were on high alert. I received a warning message, stayed put, but sat up. There was a shadow at the foot of the bed. The spirit was standing there staring at me. I could see it clearly because the moon was shining in the louvered blinds behind it. I blinking to clear my vision, the spirit took one step back, into the darker shadow of the corner. It disappeared. It was gone as far as I could see, but I could sense it was still there.

I became irritated, threw the covers back, got up and marched to the corner where this spirit stood. I stopping just short of the wall, reached out with both hands, and stirred the air. I could tell the spirit was now gone. I was covered from head to toe in goose bumps, quiet the reaction. I headed out of the bedroom to get drink of water. I needed to settle down a bit. I put the white light of protection around our room and the entire house. I also asked for Angel protection in each room of the house. As soon as I made that request, all the normal noises of our house were back. All was settled. I went back to bed.

It had been two week since the death of my dad, but it felt as emotionally difficult as if it were yesterday. People are not really prepared to lose their parents. Silly way to feel, I know, but the shock from his death made me wish someone would have warned me. My empathy overflows with new understanding for all those people who have lost a parent before me. I truly did not understand how painful it can be.

I had not dreamt of my dad nor seen him anywhere. I wondered if I was foolishly getting upset, when it was simply too soon for him. I swept at the bug or cobweb brushing my arm, again. It was annoying me, so I looked thoroughly at the area around me, and my tee shirt sleeve to make sure nothing was hanging from it. Nothing, there was nothing. As I looked at my arm, the feeling of something brushing by it happened again. There was no visible reason for this sensation.

I had been feeling if for two days, but being a, stubborn person, Chose to ignore it. I thought since it was summer, and we live on the water, spiders and cobwebs are everywhere. By the third day of this sensation, I concluded there had to something more to this. I desperately wanted it to be my dad. But, that was a huge leap.

My son, came into the house, "Wow, Grandpa has been at work with me for the last two days!"

Smiling, I asked, "What did he do?"

"He has been on the pool deck with me. I've seen him at least four times each day."

This was music to my ears and satisfying to my soul. I was extremely happy for my son. I asked him, "Do you appreciate your gift a bit more now?"

My answer was a huge hug. My son and his grandfather were incredibly close. This was proving to be a very hard time for him, as well.

"You know your grandpa assumed you would see him." Again, no verbal reply but a huge smile with water filled eyes. They were the image of his grandpa's, looking back at me. While we were talking about his grandpa, I told him about what had been happening to me. As those words left my mouth, I had the sensation again on my arm. I looked up from my arm and into my sons face. We smiled at each other. We knew who was responsible.

Later, when I was alone in the house, I thanked my dad for his gifts to us. They were wonderful. The next day my son came home from work and said, "Grandpa was not on the pool deck with me today."

I felt as sad as he sounded. We talked and concluded that he had sufficiently let us know he was fine and we were loved. He needed to move on and let others know the same. We also talked about the fact that he will visit again, when he can. This was a comfort to us both.

...Finally, I have been waiting for you...

I woke up not feeling well. I went to see the doctor. It was not a shock, when I was diagnosed with a sinus infection. When I returned home, I made a cup of tea while talking to my doggie daughter Lola. While retrieving my cup of hot water from the microwave, I turned to place it on the counter, which faces the living room. I looked across the room and spotted a shadow seated on the couch. It was the exact shape of my father, and he was sitting in the same spot he always sat on my couch. The shape was backlit perfectly from the light of the windows behind. That was the reason he sat in that spot, there wasn't a glare in his glasses from the windows.

He came to visit Lola and I. What a great feeling. I told him I was okay, just my seasonal sinus stuff. I thanked him for checking on me, told him I loved and missed him. His shadowy outline slowly faded away. As he did so, my heart broke a bit with the thought of losing him again. I took a deep cleansing breath and said to Lola, "How can I be sad when I have been given such a gift? I have to buck up and appreciate that he and I are both okay."

This was the visit I had been waiting for. I needed to get out of my own way to see it. I am amazed every day at how much I still do not know, but I continue to learn and grow

###

CHAPTER 7

GHOST AND SPIRIT EXPLORATION

I was invited to join in on a ghost hunt, well, an exploration. We were not hunting. The person that extended the invitation was a woman I met doing a local, psychic fair. There would be three of us going: she, her partner (who is an empath) and me. It took me all of about one-second to say yes, when she asked. This is something I have wanted to do for a long time.

What made this case perfect was that it was a family needing help. They were petrified by the things going on in their home. Mostly they were frightened for their daughter; because she was the one most bother by the ghosts.

I said the woman running this exploration, "You said plural?"

She said, "Because they did."

We took off and headed to a place called Grosse Ile. It was about an hour and a half drive from my house. The island sits in the mouth o the Detroit River, at the top of Lake Erie. It's a beautiful area, originally inhabited by Native Americans. It is surrounded by fast moving water. We know that all these things can cause spirit energy to amplify.

The fact that Native Americans lived and died there, kept running through my mind. I hoped their spirits would be friendly to us. Adding to the mix of this evening, it has been raining for hours and the weather had evolved into a thunderstorm. This is another amplifier of spirit activity. I could not help thinking we might be walking into a fever pitched mess. But time would tell.

Nothing outwardly seemed wrong as we arrived at their home. I looked around counted fourteen other houses on the court with theirs. The mother and daughter came out to meet us in the driveway. I liked them instantly.

As soon as I stepped into the house, I felt as if I was on a spinning ride. Dizziness hit me hard, so I grabbed onto the front door knob for stability. I was being confronted by spirits the moment I entered the house. I looked at the one psychic and said, "I am so dizzy, it hit me like a ton of bricks."

She replied, "Me too."

The mom overheard us and said, "I am as well, but it happens often. I thought it was just me." We shook our heads no. It was not simply just her. We now knew the mom is sensitive.

I could feel a head ache building. I thought it was the weather finally getting to my sinuses. It was too sudden for that, though. I did not mention this to anyone yet. I did not want to be a complainer.

The husband joined us in the hall and invited us further into the home. They seemed to be a nice, a normal family. I had wondered about that before we arrived. We had no idea what we were walking into. I bet they thought the same about us, not knowing what to expect.

We followed the family down the hall, past a formal dining area, and went into the kitchen and grate room area. It was an open concept. I was even dizzier now. It was getting worse the closer I got to the great room. The mom was now filling us in about a local ghost hunting group. They had them come in a few weeks earlier. She said it was bad. They had provoked the spirits horribly.

That came up as I was looking out at the back yard through the kitchens sliding glass door. The mom pointed to a huge tree just off the deck. It was beautiful. She said the hunting group thought the tree was haunted. I looked past the tree to the row of pine trees on the property line. I was shocked. The feeling of being watched was very strong but what shocked me was the movement within the trees. I could see shadows moving horizontal all the way along the row of trees. The shadows were moving among the trees.

I leaned my head back in the house, and informed the other two women who were with me about the tree shadows. They checked it out, and one of them whipped her head back around and looked shockingly at me. I shook my head yes, that I had seen it, too.

Next on the tour was the basement. I was the last down and, as I turned the corner and went into the main part of the basement, the other women ahead of me turned and looked at me. They had shocked looks and one had tears running down her face. She is an empath. This is someone who is sensitive to feelings and emotions of other people and spirits. I was confused because whatever they were seeing was not showing itself to me. I looked around, the basement was unfinished, and mostly storage shelves lined the walls. In the back corner, the women were looking at two assembled Christmas trees, not decorated, just stored there.

At this point, I saw my first shadow movement, against one of the basements outer walls. I looked up at one of the basement widows where I saw pasty grayish faces in the glass. They were outside. I asked, "What are you seeing?"

"We see five children around the Christmas trees. One is an infant and one a cranky, old Native American male."

I wished I could see them and was confused as to why I could not. I was feeling them and could see streaks of shadows moving around, but that was all. Then, all three of us heard a child's laughter. Our heads whipped around to look at each other. It was cool. I hoped the digital recorder we were using picked it up. I would find out several months later, it had not.

I turned to head up the stairs. I found myself rubbing the center of my chest with the ball of my hand. I had a hard time climbing the stairs, I felt very winded at the top. The stairs were not that long, so I should not have felt that way.

Back in the main foyer, we headed up stairs to the second floor. The other two women I was with hung back to talk to the mom. On the third step of the stairs, I had to sit down and put my head between my legs. I was dizzy, my chest was tight and I now had a full blown head ache. This was far from normal, spirit was trying to get me out of the house.

After a moment, I was feeling some better, so I stood up and moved up a few steps. I wanted to see if any of the others would feel what I had. They came into the foyer and started up the stairs. Not knowing what I had gone through, I watched them. The first one to head up, stopped quickly, grabbed the hand railing and said, "Wow, I am so dizzy." She was on the third step.

With each step I took toward the second floor landing, I felt less dizzy. My headache felt better, and the tightness in my chest went away. When all of us were up stairs, we went into each of the four bed rooms and two bath rooms. We commented on the amount of activity we were feeling in each of the rooms. Some had more activity then others. For me, it all felt the same up there, spirit run amuck.

The mom said there was not activity in one of the bathrooms, but I disagreed. When we all came up stairs, the spirits scattered, and went where they could. I felt them in every room on that floor. In the master bedroom, I knew there was a spirit close. I had proof when I saw a shadow move across a wall. I followed it into one of the walk-in closets. Amazed I watched as it went through the wall to the outside.

We stopped to have a discussion on the second floor landing. The discussion was about our findings and the best way for the home owners to take back their house. When we arrived back on the main floor, we sat around the formal dining room table to settle and see what the home owners were thinking. We talked about the tremendous amount of spirit activity on all three floors of the house and the whole yard. The spirit activity was not confined to just the back yard. When I entered the dining room, there were spirit faces looking in through the large window that looked out onto the side yard.

All three of us had come to the same conclusion, the daughter was a strong psychic, but had no idea she was different from anyone else. That sounded familiar! The daughter was the reason we had been called in. Her parents were justifiably worried about her. The spirits were drawn to her. Along with that attraction, came another attraction, from her deceased grandparents. They had shown up to stand with her and protect her. That is a good thing, but is a double edged sword. Spirit overload, as in this case, can open portals or vortices. This allows even more spirits to enter at their will. Those spirits can be good or bad.

One of the psychics said the daughter had two grandmothers and several other family members standing behind her at all times. This helped explain the crowded feeling I had when we came in the house. Later, on my way home, I called my husband and told him, "The house was packed with spirits. It was like the homeowners were having a huge party, but they were the only ones not invited!"

The other psychic told the family exactly who was standing with their daughter. They seemed relieved by that information. She then told them, "This is your house, you own it, take it back. You have to be as rude to them as they are to you. They will not like it, but they will go away."

The mom said, "That is odd, my head ache, just went away. Like someone just snapped their fingers and it went away."

Mine had gone away while we were upstairs and had stayed away, thankfully.

While seated at the dining room table, I was facing the main hall. I kept seeing shadows dart by behind the other two women. I watched as shadows came through the closed basement door, into the hall, toward the front door and stairs.

One of the other psychics and I decided to check the basement out again. It was just us, without any lights. I hoped this would make a difference in the activity. We quietly opened the basement door, and stepped lightly down the stairs. I am not sure why, because they knew we were coming anyway. At the bottom of the stairs, we turned left, and stepped into total darkness. I was following behind when, WHAM CLANG! I walked smack dab into one of the black, basement support poles. The first sound was my body making contact, the second was my metal rimmed glasses hitting the pole. I was totally committed and walked right into that sucker. We laughed. I admit I was a bit embarrassed.

We stopping there, and started the recorder. We stood mute for a few minutes, letting the possible effects of my "not so subtle" entrance, die down. It also gave us time for our eyes to adjust to the darkness. I noticed swirling movement between the two of us, low to the floor. It was an excited movement. The tightness in my chest was back and I felt as if someone was standing right in front of me. I talked myself into thinking that I simply ended up closer than I thought to the shelving under the stairs. I was definitely having labored breathing and noticed my dizziness had returned. I put my hand on the basement pole for support. It kept me from swaying.

I wanting to back up from the shelving unit, but did not want to let go of the pole. I was dizzy, and the swirling toward the floor was still happening. The other investigator asked me to turn the basement lights on, since I was closer, and she wanted to snap pictures just as the lights came on. I turned on the lights, and stepped back to the exact spot next to the pole I had been in the dark. I was shocked by the realization of how much space there actually had been between me and the shelving under the stairs. There had to be a good five feet. What was the solid mass that had been standing right in front of me?

My chest was no longer tight, and the dizzy feeling was gone. Now I had a bothered feeling, something had just tried to intimidate me. That made me mad. We moved further into the basement, toward the back wall. We chatted about what we saw and felt in this area. Our conversation carried over to thoughts about the rest of the house, when we simultaneously turned and looked at the basement window to my left, her right. We both said, "Spirits kept looking in that window!" We looked back at each other and smiled. That was confirmation for us both.

We went back upstairs, sat around the dining room table, and began discussing our findings.

The first question they asked was, "What was the loud clang we heard?"

Embarrassed, I admitted, "It was me running into a pole. Did I mention we were in the dark?" They were kind to me and only gave little smirking smiles. I'm sure later they had a good laugh. I hope so, I did. It was funny!

The other psychic, the empath, went to the basement for a last visit. She returned to the table after about ten minutes, sullen. She had previously mentioned little children and an infant, but nothing else. Now she told us that the children had died from and illness. The infant had also contracted this illness, but was smothered by the parents. They did this rather than have it suffer and die slowly. We were speechless.

Then she told us of the cranky old, Native American, male. She told him, "Leave the basement and stay outside. You're not nice to anyone, so, not welcome." This made me smile.

The conversation turned to the wrap up, it was time for our final thoughts and suggestions. We told them to be strong, take the house back, get their daughter to a psychic that can teach her, smudge the house and aggressively take control.

We departed going our separate ways. I was exhausted and wired at the same time. I needed my home and family. This was my first ghost exploration. We explored, got information and gave suggestions of what to do. My goal was to help the family, and I pray we did.

###

I was asked by a friend to view a new rental home she had purchased. Being a house voyeur, I went right over after my workout class. As it turns out, only one other of her friends showed up for the tour. I pulled into the driveway, and sensed instantly that there was a spirit in the house. It was looking out the window at us. I could see the spirit, but know it was there in the window.

When I walked into the house, I felt the spirit's confusion. It wondered what we are doing there. This was a very low level of energy, a laid back feel, nothing angry or crazy. I was happy for the owner and for those who would rent the house.

We toured the house and stopped to chat in the back bedroom. The owner turned to me and whispered, "Do you feel anything?" Knock me down with a feather! I had no idea this is why she asked me to come over. I was taken totally by surprise. I felt I was being used? All she had to do was be honest with me, I would have gone anyway. I wondered then if maybe she could not go so far as to ask because then she would have to semi believe in this ghost.

Feeling used and hurt, I said, "Yes, in fact I do." The smile dropped from her face, I walked out of the room, no further details given. I left the house, but I felt bad that I had been rude. My mother taught me better.

This was a learning experience for me. It taught me that ghosts and spirits are still talked about, by some people, in hushed tones. It has been brought to my attention, also, that there are people in and around my life that are friendly to me but feel disdain toward me. All of these things are what they are. People will believe what they want. I am not here to preach this to people, that is not my path. I do, however stand up for my God-given gifts and my life's path. I hope that everyone finds their joy and passion.

I replied to a friend's post on social media. The post struck me as odd, not so much for what it said, but for what it did not say. She then sent me a private massage, "Funny that you would be the first to reply. I want to ask you something."

My feeling from the post was that she needed help, spiritual help. I knew this was not going to be a laughing matter. Her next private message said, "My husband and I are seeing something, a ghost, in our home. We were wondering who it is and why it is here?"

I asked for details, "Where does it show up? How long have you been seeing it and or sensing its presence? Is there a certain time of day it shows up?"

She said, "My husband has seen her."

I thought okay, it's a female. She continued, "He said it was a woman, he saw her come up and out of the basement. She disappeared as it approached the hall that leads to the bedrooms."

I asked, "Could this be a Grandmother or his mother?" I was thinking this since they had a small child, and a grandparent spirits have been known to come visit the little ones.

She said, "Yes, my husband thinks it is his mother."

I had to agree, I felt it was his mother too. I had the distinct feeling she was beating around the bush, that there was more, but I did not want to plant ideas and possibly complicate things.

We communicated over the computer for a bit longer, and that was that. She left loads of unanswered questions, loads of unasked questions. She seemed good leaving things as they were. She must have received answers to her questions. I had to be good with it, too. I do not like to be pushy.

This is not over. I am convinced we will talk again.

As I have learned, spirit issues in the home can have strings attached. It is your home, your haven, your safe place and this intrusion is personal. It intrudes on your mind and spiritual beliefs. In a nutshell, this is not a simple thing to have happen.

I was contacted again by our friends who believe the husband's deceased mother is hanging out with them. They requested I come over to their house. We set a day that worked for all of us. We picked Good Friday. I am not sure this day's meaning will have any impact on spiritual vibration or not.

I arrived at their home, nervous and excited. I wanted to know if what I felt while talking on the phone to them was actually what was there. I had been having feelings about other situations for many months. This might be the validation I have been looking for.

I knew the family was fine. I was convinced nothing in the house was there to harm them. I was planning on making that clear, so they could relax. Being fearful is one thing, being bothered is another. Unsure I could do anything about that problem, I was sure going to try.

How will I convince them they might have to live with spirit? At the time, I thought that was a viable alternative. I have since learned, it was not. I contacted a psychic that I met on line. With permission from the homeowners, I arranged for her meet me at their home.

We arrived separately and gathered in the driveway outside the open, garage door. Only the wife was available for the meeting. We were to proceed without her husband. We were standing in a semi-circle, talking in the driveway. Just as we turned to walk through the garage into the house, there was a LOUD noise from in the garage. We looked to the home owner to see if, by change, this was normal. By the look on her face, we knew that answer without asking. The psychic and I smiled at each other, and simultaneously said, "Here we go!"

One step into the house and I felt dizzy and disoriented. It could have been the effects of the cold I knew was coming on. I had to consider that possibility. We followed the homeowner into the living room, to talk in more detail. We needed to get an idea of what they expected from us, and what they wanted us to do.

As I stood next to the psychic, our attention was drawn down between us. Something walked between us, brushing against our legs. This had to have been a cat spirit. It felt exactly like the actions of a cat getting some love and attention. We looked at each other and laughed. It was cute. I looked from her to the homeowner, she was not impressed. This was not cute to her at all.

Behind us, toward the hall, we both picked up a female spirit. I knew immediately it was the male homeowner's mom. There was no doubt in my mind. After touring the main floor, we headed to the basement. I felt odd and dizzy while on the stairs. This was only a few feet from the door we used to enter the house. I paid attention to what was happening and where. It had meaning and that would be evident, eventually. It always works out that way.

We walked about a quarter of the way through the basement, we then turned around to face the stairs. The room behind the stairs seemed to zoom into focus for me. I knew, from previous experience of this, there was a spirit back there. Just as I thought, I saw a shadow move in that area. It was a male spirit, he was simply hanging out. He liked the basement. Interesting, this is now spirit number two in the house. The male homeowner joined us. I did not wanting to frighten anyone, so I kept this information to myself.

From the basement, we headed to the second floor and a strange event occurred that ranks high on my all time weird list. We did some sensory work in the loft area of the second floor, and I felt watched. I turned to walk into the bedroom, at the far end of the loft, but could not. I was being blocked from entering the room. The psychic walked right into the room, but when I tried to follow, it was as if an unseen wall had been built. I physically could not enter the room. This had never happened before. It was weird. I took a step back, and tried to walk into the room for a second time. It felt as if plastic wrap had been put across the door as a prank. I almost bounced back when I ran into this invisible barrier. Sadly, the psychic misunderstood my actions. She thought I was afraid to enter the room. This was not the case, I promptly informed her of that.

We finally completed the whole house investigation. We both thought it would be a good idea to sage the house. After that was done, we gathered to talk. It was decided that if this ceremony did not work, a shaman would be called in.

Three days later, I talked with the homeowners on the phone. I asked if I could come back over to see how the house felt. On the way over, I tuned into the house and could feel the spirit energy. They were not gone. I hoped, however, things were quiet for the people in the house.

The wife and I sat in the living room, chatting about different things. I casually glanced around the room from where I was seated. I wondered if either of the spirits would appear for me. I was feeling spirit energy, so I focused as best I could. There was a feeling of peace, it was nice. I think part of that was the peace felt by the homeowners after the sage had been burned. I did not want them to worry, so I did not mention the current spirit energy I sensed.

In my head, I thought, okay, who are you and where are you? I moved a little in my seat to be able to see down the hall. I had a feeling that answered to the "where" question. It did not take long until I got a quick glimpse of the female spirit. She was peeking at us, wanting to know why I was back and what was happening.

I did some debunking on this visit as well. During the first visit, I walked into a passageway between two rooms. The area almost caused me to fall over. I felt disoriented. This time, I noticed some obvious causes for my disorientation. The light went from bright to dark, there were two different kinds of flooring, and the ceiling dropped and rose in certain spots. When those features were combined, it gave me the funhouse effect. This is the feeling you experience when you walk or stand on or near something you think is level, but it is not, or when your vision perceives something to be uneven by the way it looks, but it is actually the opposite.

I realized my brain was playing tricks on me during my first visit to the house. However, in the same token, with this visit, I had verified the presence of a female spirit. I told the homeowners my thoughts. They were please to hear something had been debunked.

I went up stairs to the bedroom I had been stopped from enter the first visit. We had used sage in this area and the threshold was salted. The salt would block spirit from leaving the room, assuming it was in the room. I approached the door, wondering if I would be able to get in. I opened the door and walked right in! The room was bright and energy free. Maybe the energy picked up in here before was simply residual, from a past owner's child. I told the current homeowners that there was nothing to worry about in that room anymore.

We sat back down in the living room, so we could discuss my opinion about what was currently happening. I told them, "I do not think any of the spirits here are mean. If their goal was to harm you, they would have done so already. I think the female is here to see your child and her son (the husband). I also think she is here to protect you from the male spirit that is in the basement."

They looked at each other in disbelief. That explained the feeling they always had of being watched down there. Before I left, I told them to relax, and see if they could accept the spirits. If not, we will call a shaman in to bless and cleanse the house.

###

My phone alerted me of a text from the couple in the previous event. It had been almost three weeks since I went to their house because of spirit activity. They felt it was time to bring in a shaman. They had made arrangements. The shaman would be coming within the week. They wanted to know if I would like to be there. "Hell, yes!" was my reply. I knew the haunting must have changed for them to request a shaman visit.

The day of the blessing, I arrived at the house early. The shaman requested they have their child in attendance, as well. Since she sees her grandmother in spirit form, it made sense to include her in the house blessing and cleansing. While we waited for the shaman to arrive, we all sat quietly, chatting in the living room. I could feel the inquisitive female spirit checking things out. I could also feel a male spirit but there was not much substance to him. It felt as if he was simply floating, lazy like. Surprisingly, I picked up on a new spirit in the house, another male. This male spirit feels different then the male spirit in the basement.

The shaman arrived. He asked us to join him outside. He said, "I want to talk out here, even though they know I am here, and why. I am going to do a blessing on each of you before we move inside and begin. I, too, will be blessed and ask for protection for us all."

He took out, huge hawk feathers, and holy water. He put the holy water on the feathers, and did the sign of the cross across each of us, said a blessing and asked for protection. I asked him, "Am I correct in my feeling that each of the spirits in the house is now watching us from the upper floor windows?"

"Yes, they are. They knew I was coming long before I got here."

I told him, "I could tell, the energy in there is very different then in the past."

Once back inside the house, he lit a bundle of sage. When the flames were gone and only the smoke remained, he began. He instructed the male homeowner to dip his fingers into the holy water, and make the sign of the cross over every window and doors in the house. As he applied the holy water, he had to recite a specific prayer. He told us this was to stop more spirits from entering the home, and to stop the movement of the spirits already inside. We moved as a group, from room to room. The shaman fanning the sage smoke with his feather while he said a continuous prayer.

The female homeowner asked about the purpose of the sage smoke. The shaman said, "It attaches to the spirits and as the smoke dissipates, so does the spirit." He then warned, "The spirits do not want to go and might try to attach to you. You will know if they do."

The female homeowner and I looked at each other, but I was the only one smiling. He was right, she and I both started to feel nauseated. Thankfully, the feeling passed quickly, but not until we had moved on to another area of the house. My gut told me the spirit was trapped in that area and tried to attach to us in order to get out. It was stuck.

With the main floor and second floor sagged and blessed, it was now time to move to the basement. While down there, we did a loop of the entire area. Just as the shaman said the last words of his prayer, the smoke from the sage bundle went out. He said, "We are done, did you notice what happened?"

We did, but thought nothing of it. This event was a first for all of us so we did not know what to expect. He continued, "The smoke went out just as I said the last of the prayer. If the sage had continued to smoke, I would have continued to pray. It would have meant that the spirits had not yet completely dissipated, and more work was needed."

We stood in the living room for a while, talking about our hopes of success from today's ceremony. I asked the shaman, "What spirits did you sense?"

"I sensed two males and a female. The male in the basement is a past homeowner. The female is the mother to the current male homeowner. She came for the baby, and to protect the family." He then looked at the male homeowner and said, "She is fighting to stay, she does not want to go."

I looked over at the homeowner and I knew he had been feeling this as well. He had wet eyes, this is not a man that wants you to see this side of him. But, right now, he hurt. I felt awful for him. He had lost his mom once already in his lifetime and was facing it again.

The shaman said, "You know what you need to do."

With that, the husband got up and said, "I will be back, I need to go have a private good-bye with my mom." He walked off to another part of the house. I sat there trying not to sob out loud, this was the hardest event I had witnessed in a long time. I did not want my friend to hurt, but there was nothing I could do about it.

He came back in the room and said, "That was hard."
No one spoke, we grieved with him. As we all sat quietly for those few moments, it became apparent how quiet and peaceful the house had become. It even looked like the rooms

were brighter, as a fog had lifted. As conversation started back up, we each made a statement to that fact.

The shaman's statement made me think about my own home. He said, "Spirits in your home use energy, your energy. You will notice now you have more energy than you each had. I bet you all have been tired and did not know why."

The homeowners both said, "We thought it was our overly busy schedules."

"No, you had three spirits in here and they were using you."

With that, I said, "That means I have to send the two spirits in my house packing."

The shaman looked at me, "Really? You know better and yes you do! Send them away today."

He gave me a sage bundle to burn, in case I needed it. I left for home. I wanted the homeowners to have some private time with the shaman, so they could have an open conversation with him about the day's events.

During the drive home, I felt sad and tired. I had been through way too many mood changes for one day, and still had energy work to do once I got home. I dreaded it. I knew what I had to do, but did not want to do it. However, getting our energy back would be fantastic! We did not even realize this had happened, because it was gradual. I had been physically drained of energy for at least a year. I know better.

I procrastinated, and put the eviction ceremony off until the next day. I wanted to have a private, heart-to-heart, conversation with the spirits before I asked them to go.

After my husband and son left the house the next morning, I started the conversation, "It is quite simple, you both have to go. I think we all knew this day would come. There is nothing to be frightened about in going home to God. There is nothing here on Earth for you, go home and be at peace. You do know that you have loving family and friends who have been waiting for you. It is time, you have to go."

I was amazed, and a bit sad. I could feel the energy of one of them diminishing, bit by bit, then he was gone. I said, "Thank you and God bless. You may not return to stay and will not be replaced by anyone or anything. The space shall remain empty. The way you exit will be immediately closed, and will not allow anything else in."

One down, and one to go. I knew one of the spirits remained in the house. It was my great uncle. He was going to take more work. I think the spirit of the previous homeowner was ready to go, once I explained he would be safe and people were waiting. He had been here for many years. His boy (our son) was now grown, and did not need or want his spirit around any longer.

Getting rid of my great-uncle took another three days of "down and dirty" conversations. He was afraid to leave. My impression was that he thought God and his family were mad at him. His was a heroic, and tragic, figure in history. All of which, as I told him, should only make him feel proud. In part, I think that conversation helped. I could feel my great-uncle leaving, but only a bit at a time. As I continued telling him he had no choice but to leave, a bit more of him would go. By the last day, all I could feel of his spirit was about the size of an American quarter. I knew in my gut, that if any of him remained, it left a door open. This could then not only let him back in, but other spirits as well. They could be good or bad, even alter the health of my home and family. I kept hearing from him, "See I'm gone. That is good enough, no problem."

In fact, it was a problem and I needed to take care of it. In my mind, I pictured the area in the attic I knew he resided. Then, I pictured a huge vacuum, the big canister type, sucking up all the dust and spirit debris I could imagine. Then, in my mind, I painted that entire part of the attic stark white, with a huge paintbrush. As a finishing touch, I put the sign of the cross, in white paint, over the tiny black dot that my great uncle had left behind.

After I said, "This area is close. No spirits may come and stay, or visit that area. No spirits may come and stay in any area of the house."

I thought I should finish the job so I pictured the huge vacuum out over the lake, dumping the contents into the deepest part of the lake. As a mental after thought, I dropped the vacuum in the water as well. I can always conjure another one up in my mind. That one was now unusable. I then put the white light of protection over the house, in the attic and over each of us.

That night, when I was just about asleep, I asked for an angel to come sit in the attic to make sure it was secure. I then said, "Thank you" for the entire days work."

The next night, we settled to watch television after dinner. My husband and son commented on how much better they felt all day, how much energy they had. They thought it might have been the weather or something. I thought, "Or something is right!"

Little did I realize, none of this was over yet.

Exie Susanne Smith

Our trip to Italy was simply amazing! We wanted to share pictures and stories, so we invited friends over for dinner and drinks . As we were showing the pictures via the television, I noticed shadow movement off to my right, past the kitchen down the hall,

My husband asked, "Are you all right? You just made a holy shit sort of face!"

"Sorry, yes I am fine. I saw movement in the hall. It was a very interesting looking spirit."

We quickly dropped the subject so as not to freak out our dinner guests. After they left, however, I told my husband about the new spirit that appeared in our hall way. He had his back to us. I noticed he was tall, over six feet, and big, over two-hundred pounds. He had dishwater blond hair. His shirt had short sleeves, and button down collar. It looked white, but could have been beige. I think his pants were navy blue, possibly jeans. He turned and ran down the hall toward us, freakishly fast. No human could move that quickly.

I have no idea what that was about, why he dropped in, where he came from or why he was running. But, I do know it was cool!

CHAPTER 8

STEPS TOWARD BELIEF

I have been selling my book at a monthly held psychic fair here in Michigan. The first time doing this, or any show, made me a nervous wreck. Truth be told, it took several times working this event before I was comfortable. The others working it were so kind. I did appreciate that.

While setting up for this first event, I knew I was nervous. I had not anticipated a psychic approaching my table to help chill me out! She said, "You should calm down or you will chase away customers from your table." I thanked her knowing she was right.

Once all the psychics were set up, eight in total, it felt a new sensation. It was as if the room started to hum. At one point, it felt as if someone had placed a pole in the center of the room and were now on a moving carousel ride. Slow and easy, the room seemed to glide along in a gentle circle.

Late in the day, one of the psychics asked, "Why not do readings as well as sell your book?"

"I am not gifted enough for that."

She laughed, "No you are not secure enough for that!"

This was food for thought. I went out the next day and bought a deck of tarot cards for use with the public. I have a private deck that I do not allow people to touch. I know I could clean the deck of their energy, but I like having it all to myself.

With the new deck, I have been doing free readings for friends. I am still very dependent upon the book that describes each card's meaning. Everyone that I have read for has been understanding of the fact I am new at it. I must say, however, my readings are informative and accurate. I am not sure what my future holds with these cards. I like using them and think, eventually, I could read without them. My great grandmother read tea leaves, so this sort of thing does run in the family

As the days and months tick by, and I become more familiar with my gifts, I have decided to leave the tarot cards behind. Reading the future is not where I feel my path is leading. At the moment, I am helping people by looking at the past and the present. This feels right to be what I term a "Spiritual Medium," rather than a psychic medium.

This event also takes place at a psychic fair, all be it, a much larger one. There were at least thirty gifted people doing readings, healing, etc. The fair would not start for a while, but I was ready to start meeting people and sell my book. I was sitting at my table, watching people milling about, and waiting for the fair to open. One of those people in the crowd caught my attention. A woman walked past my table, and then came back by in the other direction. When she appeared for the third time, she walked right directly over to me and said hello.

I stood up and said hello. She looking directly into my eyes and smiled. It was a knowing smile, she was there for a reason! I could feel energy rolling off of her. She was a spiritually powerful person. Casually, we chatted for a moment and then she asked, "Who is John? He is coming in very strong and deliberate."

I was drawing a blank. "I do not really know a John, not in everyday life." It finally clicked and I gave the last name of whom I thought it might be.

"Yes, that is it. Tell his wife he is always there."

Smiling, "Of course I will tell her."

I proceeded to tell her the sad story of his death and that I had helped the widow find his wedding ring.

The psychic looked at me and said, "Shut up and listen. Keep your ego in check. It will serve you better."

My initial reaction was as if I had just been spanked! I actually felt as if my left butt check was stinging.

She said, "Sometimes, I spank people with information!"

I let out a hardy laugh, but she was not kidding. I told her, "No problem, the sting will subside."

She then said, "Your spirit guide said you need to stop talking and listen. She is talking to you, believe and shut up."

As abrupt as she was, I understood what she was saying and replied, "I have been trying to talk to my spirit guide for years, asking why I could not hear her. In my mind, I think it is simply me talking to me, not anyone else. To be fair I would hear things that I could not possibly know but still did not trust it."

She asked, "Do you always talk so formally?"

"She calls me Susanne, which is formal in my world. I assumed this is how she wants our relationship to be. My family and very close friends call me Susie. For work I am Exie Susanne. I am all of those people, but always a formal Susanne from my guide."

I drank some water and continued, "You know I do listen but meditation is not for me."

It was her turn to laugh. She said, "No mediation is not your best event. You have a mind that does not shut down. Your guide said to simply be silent and learn to trust what you hear."

I thanked her for the information, it was helpful. I have waited years for this understanding, the time had finally arrived. I was ready to hear it. My heart was happy.

I thought our conversation was over, so I thanked her again, giving her an exit, if you will. She looked me in the eyes, she had more to say. "Oh and stop worrying about the cover of your next book."

You could have knocked me over with a feather. I smiled at her and shook my head. That morning, I had asked for help with the cover and title. She then went on to describe the cover. It sounded good at the time, but chose something different when the decision had to be made. There will be a light on the cover, like the physic said, but it was my graphic artist's idea. A last minute addition that made the cover perfect.

As she was leaving, she told me make sure I wrote it all down. We said pleasantries and she went to recharge before her day started. This is the kind of thing that I love about my life. I have met and conversed with so many interesting and diverse people from all over the world. Feeling blessed.

As a follow-up to the previous event, I contacted the wife to tell her about the message from her husband through the psychic. The day after the fair, I tried to call her twice, but she was not home. I left a message on her answering machine, she did call back the next day, after work.

I started, "You are not going to believe the conversation I had with a psychic! Your husband came through to her as she passed by my table."

I told her about the entire event, and she laughed. This is not the response I expected, but I liked it for her. She said, "I found out last week that I had to redo some paper work pertaining to him. I was so out of my mind right after his death that I did it wrong."

I was not surprised. I can only imagine how difficult that must have been, despite the legalities. She said, "At one point, while I was preparing the paperwork, I looked to the heavens and said if you were only here." She sadly chuckled, "I guess he was, I just did not realize it."

After we hung up, I marveled at the effort this man used, in spirit form, to get a message to his beloved wife.

Booked late for this literary event, but was glad I did soon after meeting the woman running it. I sent her an email on the outside chance she still had room in her show for one more author. Because my genre is "New Age," I am often let in so they can advertise they have all genres represented at the show. This works for both parties and I appreciate it. It was simply meant to be for us to meet and become friends. I also learned a valuable lesson during this event. Life is about so much more than book sales.

I scheduled a webcast while attending this event. We taped it the following week and it was broadcast later the next day. I met some very interesting authors, and learned about what inspired them to write a book.

I had wonderful conversation with the smart, and extremely capable, woman putting on the event. We sat and chatted during a lull in the crowd. I found out what a strong psychic she is, and about her passion for ghost hunting. Our conversation moved from topic to topic, and as we talked I had the feeling someone was standing directly behind me. I turned to look, but no one was there. I turned back around looked at the woman I had been talking to. She had a funny look on her face. I said, "I could have sworn someone was standing behind me."

She said, "It is the author at the table behind you. She is putting out strong energy. Put some protection up behind you, as well as, in front of you. It is like having a screen door to filter, out the energy."

With this woman's powers pushing at the back of me, I got a sudden headache and my chest became tight. I usually put protection around myself before a show, but I had forgotten. I find if I drape an imaginary gauze fabric as a white light of protection over myself, it helps to filter out most emotional and spiritual things.

I had talked earlier, to the woman running the event, about asthma. I returned to that subject and told her I had been diagnosed with asthma as a small child. It was totally gone by age twelve. I saw my first spirit at age twelve and it confirmed everything I was seeing and hearing. I let go of worry and fear. I think I let go of all the symptoms of asthma too! It made me wonder if I ever really had it.

This revelation shock the hell out of both of us. She suggested I meditate on that and I laughed. I am lousy at meditating. Instead, I will seek quiet, be low key and listen for answers.

I am learning to be still, inside and out. These are my next steps, I know my guide is proud of me.

I am acquiring a strong belief in myself, my gifts, and my God. This process has been a part of the steps on my path. I have always wondered what my purpose is in my being here. What is the purpose of your life time?

I am here to learn, and so are you. So, what other reasons are there for me to have come back to Earth and live another lifetime? In seeking answers, I have learned to quiet my mind and body. I have to open my eyes to really see the things I have been doing. This will show me what my passion is. What you are passionate about? What joyfully holds your attention? This is key.

Looking at my life so far, I seem to always be helping people physically, mentally or spiritually. In the last few months, I have been contacted by at least one person a week seeking assistance. Sometimes the requests are simple, and sometimes they are heavy and scary. I do not turn any of them down.

The requests for help started with a close girlfriend asking for assistance locating her recently deceased, husbands wedding band. This event opened a floodgate! I found my passion. It was using my gifts to help others.

I talk about pet visitation in my last book. I bring it up again, because it keeps happening. I love animals and have been told they have a natural attraction to me.

Heading out of the house early one morning, running late. I needed to get to the doctor's office, where they were running one last test before my dad's surgery. I walked out of the house, and realized I had left the laundry room light on. I quickly ran back into the house. I found the spirit of our past dog Bailey, standing in the hall. As I looked further down the hall, I could see Lola getting a drink of water from her dish. Bailey has been gone fourteen years now, but she is still our daughter too. I turned the light switch off, headed back out the door. "Hello Bailey. You be a good girl!"

Bailey was laid to rest in the garden, just outside our bedroom window. I see her off and on. I love that she knows it is just fine if she comes and goes. She is always welcome.

###

While exiting the bathroom in the middle of the night, movement in the mirror on the opposite wall, caught my attention. There is, what looks to be, a shoulder, walking by inside the mirror. Whoever this was, they were wearing a hospital gown that was a shade of putrid green. A color I call insane asylum green!

The next day, I tried a number of times to debunk what I saw. I tried re-creating the event by walking so that just my shoulder was in the mirror. It was too high and too big. Then, while crouching so it would be the correct height, my shoulder was too wide. I know what I saw and had to admit, there was a ghost or spirit, in my hall mirror.

I went on with my busy day, and totally forgot about the event. That is, until bedtime came around. While using the bathroom one last time, I glanced into the hall just as my husband walked into our bedroom. As he stepped around the door, I saw a hunched over old man in an awful green hospital gown. He slunk around the corner of the door, coming out of the room. The look on his face told me he thought he had gotten away with something.

Because I was in the bathroom with the light off, he did not know he was being observed. He should have felt my anger. My husband did and said, "Honey you okay?"

That brought me out of my thoughts, "Yes," was all I could say.

During my nightly prayers of thanks for a beautiful day, I also asked for angel protection in all the rooms of the house. I went to sleep. I would have a private conversation the next day, with whatever that thing was.

I stood facing the hall mirror. Talking at this thing, I told it to get the hell out of my home! It had some nerve to be in there in the first place. I told it to leave and close whatever entry it used to come in. Then, I closed my eyes and mentally checked my house for portals of entry. There was none. What I felt was that I was the entry key. Three days before, I had mentally closed a portal in a friend's home. My rookie mistake was passing through to the other side of the portal, trying to drag a bothersome spirit with me. I jumped out of the portal, not thinking something may have come with me.

The portal was successfully shut. However, I found out that things can come in with you. I do have my sage handy, in case I need to smudge my home. Time will tell on that, and, to be honest I might do it anyway. It can't hurt.

###

CHAPTER 9

EVENTS OF OTHER PEOPLE

In the last few years, since publishing my first book, I have met and conversed with a myriad of wonderful people. During our conversations almost every one of them has had a paranormal event and is happy to share it with me. It touches my heart that they trust me enough to open up and tell me something they might not have told anyone else. It is a leap of faith and I know that.

The following are events that people have personally shared with me. With their blessing, I am happy to add them here. My reasoning for including them in this book is for other people to realize they are far from alone in having experiences.

###

Follow Your Conscious

I wrote a post on my social media page talking about a paranormal event. It got the attention of a women I workout with. She walked directly over to me before class and said, "We need to talk after class."

I have to say, I was intrigued by this request. We had talked casually in class, but not a lot. Once our workout was over, we talked in hushed tones. She said, "I have to be careful, this is a touchy subject in my line of work. I'm a real estate agent!" I did not know that and agreed with her, by nodding my head. Where was this conversation going? I also knew that she has a psychic gift. I could sense it.

She confirmed my feelings when she said, "As a person with a gift, you know what you feel when you walk into a space. So do I." She stopped talking and simply stared at me. She wanted to see my reaction, of course.

I looked back and said, "I thought as much!"

She smiled and continued, "I am conflicted. In the state of Michigan, the seller does not have to disclose the fact their house is or could possibly be haunted. When I walk into a home with a family and they fall in love with the house, but I feel something bad, what do I do?"

Coldly I told her, "You have no legal obligation of disclosure, follow the law. I know you would wrestle with your conscious and lose. This puts you between a rock and a hard place. If you do say something, anything, you put yourself out of business and will be branded a crazy lady. Not sure it is worth risk."

"If I feel evil, I will have to say something to my client."

I agreed with her on that because she could be putting someone in danger.

We talked a bit more on other subjects, one being that there are probably more spirits in locations than not. That brought a point to mind and I said, "You know, some hauntings are of the land and not of the house itself. That is what the case was with my childhood home."

We left workout, and I did not see her again for a couple of weeks. When I did, she told me, "A house I sold recently has had increase activity what should I have them do?"

"I would sage or smudge the house and have it blessed. They need a shaman."

She conveyed the message and they did as I suggested. It seems things in the house have been quiet. Everyone is happy!

My Daughter and the Nice Man

The person who experienced this event states, "I have always had paranormal experiences in my life. I expect it and say oh well."

This event is about the first time I realized my daughter was having the same type of experiences as I have had. When she turned two years old, I left my husband because of physical abuse, and had temporarily moved in with my father. I needed to save up some money, so we could get a place of our own. Meanwhile, I slept on the living room couch. Sometimes, at night, I would hear someone in the hallway outside my daughter's room. From where I was sleeping, I could see down the hall, and no one was there. I would go back to sleep.

My stepmother was hearing the walking in the hall, as well and asked me what I was doing at night. I explained to her that it wasn't me, but these things seem to happen around me.

I told her she shouldn't be scared. It's just the usual paranormal stuff.

My daughter would sometimes repeatedly sing, Twinkle, twinkle little star, at night. Occasionally I could hear her talking, but mostly she sang. Once in a while, she got out of bed, but in the morning I always found her tucked safely back in.

One day, while picking up in her bedroom, I found a man's watch. I thought she had somehow taken my dad's watch. I tried to return it to him, but it wasn't his. Next time my brother came over to the house for a visit, I tried to return it to him but again, it wasn't his. I finally thought to ask my daughter where she got the watch. She said, "From the man who visited."

Apparently she would wake up in the night and he would be there. She would sing to him and he in turn made her feel safe. Now twenty years later, we both still remember those visits from the man. It's a good memory for her, because he was a nice man.

I still don't understand why he left his watch behind, but I do love that he made my daughter feel safe.

Grandfather

In 1960, when I was eleven years old, we moved in with my grandfather to help care for him. We lived there until we could sell his house and find something different.

Not too long after we moved in, my grandfather passed

away. At the time, I was in the room I shared with my sister, getting ready for bed. I got into bed, laying there looking around, when I caught movement at the foot of my bed. I raised my head to see what it was. It was my grandfather, sitting on the foot of my bed. I gasped and stared at him, but he never looked at me. He simply bent down, pulled off his shoes and socks, and then tucked his socks into his shoes.

I leaped out of bed before he could lay down next to me. I told my sister to move over in her bed. I jumped over her, so I faced the wall, pressed my nose against it. I stayed that way all night.

My grandfather never appeared after that, which was fine, because it really scared me.

Nana Comes to Visit

In 1999, my husband and I moved into a new house. Well, it was new to us but it was actually ten years old.

One day, while my husband was at work, I sat in the den, searching through cookbooks for something new to make for dinner. Having come across one that sounded tasty, I took the book into the kitchen to get cooking. When that was done, I went back into the den to finish a chapter of the novel I was reading. Just as I entered the room, I saw movement out of the corner of my eye. I looked up find my Nana walk from the laundry room into the kitchen. I was startled, but not afraid. As she went past me, she turned her head toward me and smiled. I don't remember if I smiled back. She continued to walk for a bit, and then was gone.

I do not remember how much time went by, but she visited again. Again, I had dinner on the stove. I walked from the family room, through the kitchen, to the computer room, and happened to glance over at the stove. My Nana was standing at the stove, stirring a pot. Again, she turned her head and smiled at me, and then disappeared. This time, I felt only comfort in her presence. It wasn't scary.

I saw my sweet Nana one more time. During this last visit, she stood in my kitchen with her back to me. She didn't turn and look at me. I was standing there looking at her. She faded away, and never appeared again.

Funny that she would appear while I was cooking dinner. She had been the winner of many Betty Crocker Cooking Awards throughout her life. She obviously loved to cook.

The mere thought of her visits brings a feeling of comfort and love.

Sisterly Love

In my first book, I wrote dedications to family and friends. One of those was to my girlfriend Chris. Sadly, she was taken from us shortly after the book was finished. I had a copy set aside for her. I thought maybe one of her sisters would like to have it and called.

I contacted the sister who had been living with her before she became sick. I asked her if she would like to have Chris's copy of my book. She thought that would be great, I mailed it off to her later that day.

A couple of days later, her sister texted me, "I do the same thing with slot machines! They have to speak to me or I don't play them."

I thought aha! She not only got the book, but has read it. She was referring to a section in the book about gaming and how I can sense things with slot machines, and a bit with roulette. It dawned on me later, that slot machine story in the book takes place with her sister.

I related that to her in a text, how I thought it wild she would relate to a story that pertained to her sister. Minutes later, I received a text back from her. All it said was, "I had a visit from her yesterday."

I replied, "You did? How wonderful that she came back for you. She was here a few days ago. Showed me her portrait in ornate, wooden frames." I had never seen these photos of her. The next day, her son posted one of those pictures of her, on his social media page.

I also asked, "How did she come back to you?"

"Chris's dog, Moosie, has been sick and was up several times in the night to go outside. After letting him out the last time, I fell asleep in the chair next to the door. I was awaken by Chris's voice saying HELLLLOOO! You know, like she always did. She sounded happy."

This choked me up.

She continued, "I have never come awake faster or more completely. Moosie was crying at the door for me to let him in. When I did, he went to the entrance of the living room and stood there. I noticed the room was glowing from the computer screen, which I know I turned off. The room was glowing really bright. I knew this was more than the computer screen."

"That had to have been an amazing feeling, did you go in the room?"

She replied, "Moosie wanted to, but didn't. He simply stood there, now next to me, and cried. I was so tired, I just want to go back to bed!"

I said, "It seems to me he knew something was up."

"Yup, he did, but he is kind of a chicken. I had told Chris to contact me if she could. Wouldn't you know it, she does and it's about the dog."

I replied, "That is all understandable, however, I think this was all about you. She smartly used the dog to get your attention. She is close, just in a different form."

Wonderful job, Chris, you fulfilled your sisters request.

A Fathers visit

My daughter's father passed away suddenly in 2004. We moved into my current home a year later. After being here for a few months, I was home alone one night, watching television. Suddenly, a voice reached out to me in my mind. I didn't hear the tone, but knew instantly that it was my deceased ex-husband. He said, "I want you to know I am proud of her."

Our daughter had graduated high school earlier that year, so I assumed that is what he was referring to.

I replied, "I know and I am really proud of her, too."

He continued to talk, "She has become a wonderful woman. I need for you to tell her I said these things and she needs to know I will always protect her."

In my mind, I am thinking, really? Like she would ever believe this whole story?

He said, "It is important that she gets this message."

This time, I did say to him, "She will never believe me and I don't want to look crazy to her. She took your death very hard and is still tender. I do not want to bring up those hurts again and make her mad." I was arguing with a dead man, in my living room.

What he said next blew me away! "Tell her about the thing I gave her and she keeps in her car, under the seat."

"What thing?"

"I cannot tell you. I promised her I would never tell. It is our secret. Just tell her I know it is still there. Also, that I love her and will always protect her."

In the past, I have tried to talk to my daughter about this type of subject and honestly, she thinks I am crazy. That is the frame of mind I had going into this conversation with her. I had no reason to think any different.

The next night, I went to her bedroom and told her we

needed to talk. As expected, when I start to tell her that her dad came to see me, she actually asked if I had been drinking. I had not. I could tell she was starting to get angry with me so I said, "Look, he told me to tell you about something in your car that he gave you. He knows you still have and keep under the seat."

I will never forget how she looked at me. It was a combination of shock, surprise and hurt. "Do you know what I am referring to?"

She immediately started to cry and nodded yes.

"Would you tell me what it is?"

"No, it's a secret."

We hugged and I repeated everything her dad and I talked about. Our relationship, where this is concerned, is better. I am happy about that.

I have to be say, I really did want to go out and look in her car, but I didn't. I never will.

###

Grandmother Babu

My grandmother and I were very close. She was the glue to our large family. It was about a year after her death, when the image of the Virgin Mary came to me in a tanning booth. Along with the image came Babu. She wanted to tell me that I was going to be all right and everything was going to work itself out. She told me not to worry.

She was in my head, my mind. I could understand every-thing she, said plain as day. I replied out loud to her, about my financial difficulties, and she replied in my mind. Over and over she told me not to worry, I would make it through. This back and forth conversation lasted at least five minutes.

She still comes around every now and then to see how I am doing, and to reassure me that she is still with me. I feel bad because a couple of times she has come into my mind to chat, and I have to say, not now. You simply cannot hold a conver-sation, while in a group of people, with an unseen person!

The Man

My daughter and I were living in an apartment in Rochester Hills, Michigan. The place was laid out oddly. There was a hallway that ran the entire length of the apartment. In that hallway, every now and then, I would see the shadow figure of a man, in a stovepipe hat, simply walking down the hall.

The first few times it happened, I thought I was seeing things. It must be shadow play from car headlights out the window. After thinking about this, I ruled that out, no light from out of doors could actually reach the hallway.

Over time, I simply accepted that he was there. He never did more than walk down the hall. I said hi to him once, and asked if he could enlighten me about why he was here. I said, "Did you follow me here from my last place?"

It finally occurred to me the shadow man was following me

around the apartment. He would be in my way in the middle of the night when I went to use the bathroom. I would say excuse me to him, and hello again! This continued until I moved.

A Healer's Tale

I have been blessed with the gift of healing. I am a masseuse and do this as a cover for my healing work. Some people simply want a feel good massage, but more often than not, people come because something, someplace on their body is bothering them.

I am careful about making it know that I heal, even thought I use it frequently in a massage session. It scares me to think that someone might think I am crazy.

Recently, I have been researching and studying up on crystals, the different kinds and their purposes. I find it all very interesting. A few months ago, my husband bought a bag of rose quartz stones. I thought they were pretty, so we placed them all around the house. We didn't know yet exactly what they would do for us. We placed one on each night stand and as we retired for the night, would hold the stone and say our gratitude's.

The full moon was coming, so we placed the quartz stones out so they could charge back up with energy. The next day, I put them back around the house where they had been.

A woman, whom I had worked on previously, booked a message. Since I had seen her before, I was aware of the issues she had going on with her body. A session with her drained my energy. Concerned that she might need more help then I could give her, I decided to ask the Universe, God and Angels to increase my abilities and insight to better serve her.

Four days before this appointment, I was out mowing the lawn, and rushing a bit to get done before my husband got home from work. I was in such a hurry, I stopped paying attention to what I was doing and ran out of gas. For the life of me, I could not get that darn mower started again. No matter what tricks I tried, it would not start. I was getting frustrated, and that is when I hurt my neck.

The pain was so severe. It radiated like a pounding hammer from my neck. Nothing I tried worked to lessen the pain. I even tried a left over prescription for pain from the dentist. Early in the morning, my husband was getting ready for work. I was still in bed but though I should get up to see how I felt. I spotted the gems on the counter that had yet to be put back in place. I thought I would put them back around the house to get my mind off myself.

This did not help. I was exhausted, so I went back to bed. As I rested, I saw the stones on the nightstand, picked them up and placed them on my neck. I thought, why not? Maybe this will help me.

Instantly and shockingly, the pain felt as if it was being drawn from my body and within fifteen minutes, I was almost pain free. I dozed off and woke up a while later, exhilarated and excited at my find. I now knew I was going to be able to help the woman with all the physical problems, and just in time for her appointment was tomorrow.

With my client comfortably on the table, I cautiously asked how she felt about me incorporating crystals into the massage.

I told her I would be placing the rose quartz on areas while I messaged and worked on other areas. She said, "Fine." I am glad she was open to a new idea.

The quartz was working beautifully. It was taking away the pain wherever it was placed. As I thought we were about finished, my client confided in me about another area that had been very painful, but she had not wanted to say anything. I moved the quartz crystals to that area. With my healing hands and those crystals, her pain was lessening. She had tears in her eyes and said, "I can hardly feel any, oh wait, the pain is gone!"

I texted her the next evening to see how she was doing. She replied that she was doing wonderfully. I have to believe that the entire event and issues with my neck were about learning, opening my eyes to the healing and the added benefits crystal work brings to my healing practice.

The future is very exciting with this discovery. It has opened my eyes and expanded my healing abilities. I know I have more to learn.

###

GLOSSARY

Angel:
Spiritual being that assists God. There are good and evil angels. The Greek meaning is messenger of God.

Astral Projection/Travel:
Is also known as an "out of body experience." The soul leaves the physical body and travels to the astral planes or also called vibrational planes. The planes are said to be between heaven and earth.

Demon:
An evil spirit which can cause problems, trouble or unhappiness.

Demonic:
This refers to something that is done by a demon or refers to the presence of a demon.

Debunk:
To show or prove something as false. That something cannot be as claimed or to discredit.

Dreams:
Sensations, emotions and pictures that happen in your mind, most actively, during rem sleep.

Exie Susanne Smith

Ectoplasm:
A substance that is said to come out of a psychic medium during a reading or while they are in a trance. This substance is then said to become/manifest into a spirit.

Empath/Empathic:
Being sensitive to, the receiving of or feeling directly the emotions of another person or group of people.

Essence:
What each of us is made up of, our soul.

Frequency:
The level or plane on which our essence/soul vibrates.

Funhouse Effect:
The feeling you experience when you walk or stand on or near something/someplace that you perceive as being level but it is not. Thus making you feel dizzy, disoriented or off balance.

Ghost/Earthbound Spirit:
Souls who have not, for a variety of reasons, completed their transition from the living world to the afterlife.

Haunted:
Unexplainable activity occurring in any location, including the ground itself.

Haunting:
The habitual manifestation of energy in a certain location.

Ley Lines:
Invisible lines around the globe that run between important places that are thought to have power or allow spirit travel.

Lucid Dreaming:
The occurrence is basically the same as an out of body experience: the feeling that you float not walk and have contact with spirits on another plane and that you are fully aware you are dreaming.

Malevolent:
Wanting to do evil to someone.

Manifestation:
The shape and appearance of a spirit or ghost when they appear.

Mist:
A spirit or ghost, human or animal, can manifest in this way. Can signify a gathering of spiritual energy just before manifestation.

Portal:
An entrance, doorway or gate from one plane to another.

Prophetic Dream:
Seeing and event before it happens. An example: to see an event in a dream before it happens.

Reincarnation:
The soul, upon death, comes back to earth from the afterlife to a new body.

Salt:
In a spiritual context is used to chase away, protect from or ward off evil

Shadow People:
They appear to be a solid mass that is opaque or translucent. They can appear in the shape or silhouette of a human, a person you know. They show up the color of black or varying shades of. No discernible features, other than the outline shape. Because it appears in a shade of black does not mean it is evil.

Shaman:
A person, male or female, who acts as an intermediary between the natural/living world and the spirit world.

Smudging:
A cleansing technique, with Native American roots, where a dried herb bundle or sweet grass is burned for purification. Keeping an attitude of love and good intention.

Speaking In Tongues:
Utterances approximating words or speech usually produced during states of intense religious experiences.

Spirit:
Souls that have transitioned from the living world to the afterlife, that have crossed over and then returned for whatever reason.

Spirit Attachment:
When a spirit attaches itself to another person or inanimate object.

Spiritual Energy:
Consciousness manifested as energy.

Spiritual Vortex:
Cross points between energy fields in the earth's grid system or ley lines. Which can create the look of a whirlpool.

Totem:
A natural object, insect or animal that is believed to have spiritual significance and then is adopted as their symbol.

Vibratory Spirit Energy:
See Frequency

Vortex:
A mass of rapidly whirling fluid, air or mist.

White Light of Protection:
The space within the universe what positive energies are stored. This light is called upon for protection from negative energies. Similar to an Angelic light.

ABOUT THE AUTHOR

EXIE SUSANNE SMITH is a Spiritual Medium, Energy Reader, Speaker and Best Selling/International Author. Her daily life has Spirits and Ghosts coming to call no matter where she happens to be. Her first book, Welcome To My Para"Normal" Life, became a bestselling book, and, has sold around the world.

Exie's goal is to continue her education about the paranormal, in the hope of being able to better help you with honest and intelligent answers.

Exie Susanne resides in Michigan with her much loved and appreciated family.

Made in the USA
Lexington, KY
26 July 2019